Shyness and Soci

Eliminate Negative Self Talk, Relieve Stress, Overcome Your Fears, Increase Your Self-Confidence & Social Skills Using Cognitive Behavioral Therapy & Powerful Techniques

By

Stuart Killan

Stuart Killan

Contents

Stuart Killan

Your Free Gift

As a way of saying thank you for downloading. I'm offering a free bonus report called *7 Habits of Highly Confident People* that's exclusive to the readers of this book.

Get instant access at http://freeconfidencebook.com

Inside the book you'll discover

- Secrets of The Joker, and why he should be admired
- The one thing confident people *always* do first when confronted with a tough situation – learning this alone can 10X your self esteem
- How to use vision boards to achieve your goals
- Identifying your "hidden talents" – even if you don't think you have any
- The one trait you must MURDER if you are to become successful
- How to never doubt your own abilities again
- Michael Jordan's #1 success secret
- The 4 most dangerous words in your vocabulary (if you're saying these regularly you are killing your own confidence)
- How to succeed as an introvert in an extrovert's world

Download for free at http://freeconfidencebook.com

Dating for Introverts

Eliminate Approach Anxiety and Confidently Speak to and Get Dates with the Most Beautiful Women

By

Stuart Killan

Introduction

Thank you for purchasing this book, *Shyness: Eliminate Approach Anxiety and Confidently Speak to and Get Dates with the Most Beautiful Women.*

Many men often imagine the worst and do not approach the woman they want to speak to. What they fail to understand is that it is all in their heads. Unless they approach the woman, they are never going to know how she feels.

It is not unusual to be shy when you approach a woman, but that should not stop you from interacting with her. This book will help you understand when to approach a woman, and what you can say to get her attention. It is not difficult to be a nice man, but it is difficult to know exactly what you should do. You must bear in mind that you cannot become confident overnight.

Every chapter of this book will help you understand how you should approach any situation based on the outcome. This is the bridging mindset, where you accept that you are not very confident and slightly anxious and yet you decide to approach a woman.

Over the course of this book, you will learn when to approach a woman and how to make conversation with her. You will also learn how to take rejection and how you should feel if a woman does not want to speak to you. Do not put yourself down since that will not help you on your journey.

I hope the information in this book eases your anxiety and helps you approach your woman with confidence.

Chapter One: The Setting

It is difficult to approach a woman in public for many reasons. For example, she may want to be alone or she could be waiting for a group of friends. There are some places you should avoid approaching a woman, like the grocery store or the gym, where a woman goes to be by herself.

Most men are worried about approaching a woman in public; however, they are making it harder on themselves by overthinking. This chapter provides some tips on how you can approach a woman in public.

Always Walk Tall

An easy way to approach someone is by displaying outward confidence. To do this, you should approach women by walking tall. Do not slouch when you walk, but stand up straight and approach the woman with your head held high. You can copy icons like Humphrey Bogart and Clint Eastwood when you start off. This approach will show the woman that you are confident, even if you are not too confident about your play. You can practice this walk at home before you head out for your first date.

Approach Her Immediately

Have you ever stood on the sidelines and asked yourself whether the pretty lady across the hall noticed you or not? Well, she did. It is because of this that it is important that you approach a woman immediately in public. When you wait for a long time, you will come off as a 'creep' although you did not mean to. Take a breath, muster up the courage, and walk over to her. At first, it is hard to face rejection, but remember that you are never going to win the lottery if you do not buy a ticket. It is better to approach the woman sooner rather than later. You do not want to be like Alex or Rosie from the book *Where Rainbows End*.

Stop Overthinking

One of the benefits of approaching a woman immediately is that it prevents you from overthinking. You have a specific objective when you approach a woman—strike up a conversation, generate some interest, and make her want to talk to you. If you've ever worked in sales, you know that every email you write must keep the reader hooked. This is the approach you should take when you meet a girl. You do not want her to fall in love with you; you only want her to talk to you. Therefore, keep the conversations light and funny.

Use Your Body Language

When you talk to your friends, you do not face each other fully. However, when you approach a woman it must be from the side, or shift to the side after you have approached her. You should try talking to her over your shoulder and turn in when you want to say something to her. When she wants to speak to you, turn away slightly. This is a natural way to talk to her. Most men speak to a woman as if they are at an interview.

Getting Her Number

When you approach a woman in a place that is not a club or bar, tell her that you want her number because you want to meet her sometime soon. Hand your phone over and ask her to type her number in. Text her something funny like, "This is Adam, the smartest guy you have met all day!"

How to Deal with External Factors

When you approach a girl in public, there are going to be many people who will be observing you, but that should not worry you. Why worry about what others think? If you have made eye contact with the girl you like, walk up to her and speak to her. Do not worry about whether the people in the store will worry that you are a creep. Be confident and approach the girl without worrying about anything.

What Should You do if a Woman Rejects You?

If you are a guy with low confidence, you will tell yourself that you are a loser and no woman in the world will agree to date you. This is a horrible thing to tell yourself. You should remember that there are many women in the world, and there are some who will like you for who you are. Do not approach a woman with overconfidence. You cannot think that a woman will talk to you just because you think you are smart. She must also think you are smart.

If one woman rejects you, all you need to do is wait it out and approach another. You should

Stuart Killan

stop being hard on yourself and stick to the bridging mindset.

Chapter Two: How to Start a Conversation

Most men make the mistake of starting a conversation with a topic that bores women. It is true that some women love sports and politics, but you cannot expect them to be impressed by your opinion on why some people should not play sports. The obvious thing is that you should not bore a girl when you talk to her for the first time. Everybody knows this and yet men sometimes do still bore women. Why do you think that is? The reason is that men often *think* women want to hear something, but that is *not* often what women want to hear.

Find Out What She is Interested in

Some women read *Cosmopolitan* and know what topics interest men most. When you are on a date, a woman may bring up a topic that interests you, but this does not mean that you should drone on and on and bore her to death. Yes, some of the information you share will be interesting, but some of it may want her to jump off a bridge.

Before you delve into long-winded tales, try to find out what your date likes to talk about. An easy way to do this is to just ask her. Based on her expression, you will know if you have the green signal or not.

Ask Her What She Likes

How do you know if a girl is interested in the topics you choose, and how do you handle it if she tells you she is not interested? When she says, "Yes, sometimes," but does not show too much interest, change the topic immediately. But, if she says, "Oh my God, yes! I have been following them my whole life," you have a winner. Take a look at the conversation below:

You: "How often do you travel? Where's the last place you went?"

Her: "I really should travel, but I just can't find the time."

You: "Yeah, it can be hard. What else do you like to do?"

Now that she has told you that travel does not interest her, you cannot tell her about this amazing travel story you had in mind. Since you do not want to bore her, change the question and ask her what other things she likes to do. You must ensure that you frame the question in a way that will make her think. If you simply asked her what she did for fun, she can sound rebellious or cool and tell you that she either works all the time, or does not usually have fun. It is therefore a good idea to ask her a question that will make her sound uncool if she does not have an answer.

So, when you ask her questions like, "What do you do to keep life fun?" she must give you an answer that will make her look cool. These questions ensure that she invests some time in the conversation, and it shows that you want to get to know her better.

Do Not Brag

It is a known fact that women do not like it when men constantly brag about themselves. It is also important to remember that it is a waste of time to try to impress women. Instead, you should make yourself look valuable by trying to increase your worth. The problem here is that you may try too hard, and these actions will seem like you are bragging about your qualities.

It is bad to brag about yourself for the following reasons:

- When she shows some interest in you and you begin to brag, she will think that you are way out of your league. Since she is insecure about herself, she will reject you without thinking twice.

- If she does not desire you, it means she views herself as being more aware and experienced. If you brag about yourself, you strengthen her belief that she is more experienced than you are, and will enjoy watching you go out of your way to impress her.

So, what should you do to increase your value?

Always focus on the fundamentals. Women can see right through your actions. If you did not impress her when you first met her, it will be hard to impress her when you go out on a date. Women are not interested in how you talk about yourself; they are interested in how you conduct yourself.

Make Your Intentions Clear

Women are not only emotional, but are also practical. When a woman is speaking to someone, she asks herself, "Why am I talking to this person?" And if she does not find a good reason, she will excuse herself and leave. If you are approaching women for the first time, you will worry about a woman avoiding conversation by telling you that she must:

- Go back to work

- Find her friends

- Use the restroom

- Go back to class

A woman is not rejecting you when she tells you this. She is unsure of what your motives are. Because of this, you should be direct with her. Let us look at the following conversation.

You: "Hey, is this seat taken?"

Her: "No."

You: "I'm really glad it finally stopped raining!"

Her: "Yeah, me too." (*She is wondering what the point of the conversation is.*)

You: "How's that sandwich?"

Her: "Great."

You: "My favorite thing here is the club sandwich. Ever ordered that before?"

Her: "Yes, I have."

You: "Where do you work that you ended up here for lunch?"

Her: "Sorry, but I have to get back to work. Nice meeting you."

You: "It was great to meet you too."

Did you know what you wanted? Neither did she. It was a weird and awkward conversation, and the girl wanted to get out of there. Most people make this mistake, and they make women wonder why they are having a conversation with them. Women eventually leave because they feel awkward, so ensure that you make your intentions clear. Be direct, open, and honest with her.

What Should You Do if she Rejects Your Advances?

There are some people who are extremely confident about themselves. They believe that they have so much to say that any woman will be happy to talk to them. Other people are constantly worried about what they will say to a woman if she chooses to talk to them. You should strike a balance in between these mindsets. Tell yourself that there are many topics to choose from, and you can maintain a decent conversation with a woman. You may fail a few times, but once you get the hang of it, you'll know what to say to hold her attention.

Chapter Three: How to Work on Shyness

It is not unusual to be shy, but it makes it difficult for you to approach the woman you have a crush on. From the last two chapters, you know when you should approach a girl and what you should do to strike up a conversation. This chapter gives you some tips that will help you meet the woman of your dreams. When you confront a fear or problem, you will find that you can overcome them with ease.

Engage Strangers

Talk to people at stores. No, you will not come off as a creep for making casual conversation with someone. One of the best ways to overcome shyness is by increasing your comfort with casual conversation. You can approach many people and interact with them in a pressure-free and pleasant environment. This will help you develop confidence. For example, you can approach a customer service associate at any store and ask them for help or for their opinion about a product. The objective is to be polite and brief. You do not want to start a long conversation with people you do not know. You are trying to accustom yourself to talking to strangers.

Have Small Interactions

Once you have the confidence to hold brief conversations with strangers, you can start conversing with people who are not the girl you have a crush on. It is better to start with other people to reduce the pressure or fear of rejection. For example:

- Speak to people when you are at a social gathering or at work, but not to the girl you have a crush on. Practice making conversation.

- If you are at a party, approach someone and ask them where the host purchased the food or drink.

- Approach a colleague or a classmate and try to include some anecdotes when you speak to them. You might tell them about a project you're working on.

When you practice a conversation in a pleasant environment, you can overcome your fear of rejection. This will help you become more confident when you talk to people.

Make Eye Contact

When you smile and make eye contact, you will seem friendlier and more approachable. Do not constantly look into a person's eyes when you talk to them because that can be unnerving; however, make eye contact occasionally to show them your confidence. It may be difficult at first to smile and look people in the eye. Women find it attractive when you appear friendly. Smiling also helps you feel better about any situation you are in. Numerous studies have shown that smiling makes you feel confident and happier since it releases feel-good chemicals.

Embrace Your Shyness

Regardless of how much you practice, you're going to be shy when you speak to the girl you like. Do not worry about being nervous in front of her. Instead of shying away from the conversation, use your nervousness to begin a conversation with her. You can say something like, "I usually am nervous when I talk to such a beautiful girl." That will stick with her and will make sure she talks to you. Ensure that you use the tips mentioned in the previous chapter about the type of conversation you should have with her.

Be Yourself

People often like to act like somebody they are not. If you are a nice guy, be a nice guy. You do not have to pretend to be a bad boy just to make conversation with the girl you like. You will not come off as being cool or confident when you pretend to be someone else. It is important to remember that you should base any relationship on honesty. If she rejects your advances, swallow your pride and sadness, because you did not pretend to be someone you were not. If it did not work out with the girl you approached, there is certainly someone out there who will like you for you. Be patient.

Practice at Home

To overcome your shyness, practice conversations with people at home. You can stand in front of the mirror and learn to introduce yourself or greet someone with a smile on your face. When you practice regularly, the greeting or introduction becomes muscle memory. This makes it easier for you to greet a stranger since you know what you should say and how you should say it. Ensure that you practice in front of the mirror to see what you look like.

Change How You View Rejection

You are shy because you fear rejection. It is natural for someone to take rejection to heart, but instead of taking it personally, realize that rejection is a learning experience. Rejection often has less to do with you, and more to do with the other person. There are days when women will be in a bad mood or dealing with something terrible. They may also be insecure when they need to deal with others.

It is important to remember that rejection is not the end of the world. If you change your perception, you will learn to embrace rejection. You can learn from the experience and understand how you should interact with other people.

You Cannot Predict the Future

You may often try to predict the future and assess how a situation will turn out before you experience it. Human beings always imagine the worst that can happen to them. This is a way for us to survive. It is difficult to overcome this trait when you are in a situation where you are not in danger. Stop trying to analyze the million things that can go wrong when you approach a girl. Focus instead on how well it can go. You will come off as a confident person.

Chapter Four: When Should You Avoid Approaching a Girl

It is important to know when you should not approach a woman. It is nerve-wracking to approach a woman, but it becomes worse when you approach her when she does not want company. Women all over the world have stories where they were harassed by men who wanted to say hello and invaded their personal space, especially when they wanted to be left alone. If you do the same thing, she will call you a creep and probably walk away.

When She Does Not Want to be Bothered

It is important to remember that men and women communicate differently. The former are taught to directly make their wishes known, while the latter communicate their interests and desires subtly. Women rely on non-verbal communication when they interact with men. If a woman wants to be approached, she may look at you, look away, and look back at you. If she does not want to be approached, she will let you know in the same way!

For example, when a woman does not want you to approach her, she will not make eye contact with you or with anybody in the room. She may stare straight ahead, stare into her phone, look down, zone out, or look anywhere but at one person in the room. These signs mean that she does not want anybody to approach her. She can also use sunglasses or a hoodie to avoid looking at anybody.

If she is wearing earbuds or headphones, you know she does not want you to approach her. She may not be listening to music, but she does not want to be disturbed.

Public Transport

Never approach a woman if she is using public transport. People already wish they were anywhere but on the train, or bus, so it is best to avoid speaking to a woman when she is traveling. All she wants to do is get where she's going as fast as possible, without interacting with people.

If you want to approach the cute girl on the bus, you should be aware that you are approaching someone who is already suffering. You are not a creep, but she does not know that. She wants to get off the bus without having to deal with another guy who thinks that a woman on the bus has signed up for a speed dating service. Do not speak to a woman who is taking public transport. She has her guard up and does not want to talk to you. If she is interested, she will make the first move.

Remember the signs from the previous section? Keep those in mind when you are using public transport. If a woman is reading or is listening to music, do not speak to her.

At Work

When you approach a woman at work, she will be nice to you because her job demands that of her. You may want to ask the cute barista out on a date, but, remember this—she is often nice to you because you are a customer. Waitresses or bartenders may only nice to you because they want you to tip them. Unfortunately, many people misunderstand these signs, and assume that the woman is into them, so make sure that you do not make the wrong move.

Conclusion

If you are shy, it is difficult to speak to a girl without stuttering or making a fool out of yourself, but do not worry. The fear is only within you. If you build some confidence, you can speak to the girl you have a crush on without stuttering. This fear is present because you are worried about rejection. You are also worried that people will think of you as a failure, but what you should remember is that there are a lot of women out there who will be happy that you went and spoke to them.

I hope the information in this book helps you overcome your fear and helps you speak with confidence to the woman you like. Good luck!

Cognitive Behavioral Therapy

How to Free Yourself from Your Inner Monologue and Eliminate

Negative Self Forever

By

Stuart Killan

Introduction

I want to thank you for purchasing the book, 'Shyness: How to Free Yourself from Your Inner Monologue and Eliminate Negative Self-Talk Forever.'

Everybody, including the most successful people, often have a voice in the back of their head telling them that they are not good enough. We do not talk about it since we are afraid that people will think of us as weak individuals. It is easy for people to tell you to live in the present and not overthink. But, what do they really mean by that?

The only way one can achieve happiness is by altering how they perceive themselves. You can never believe someone when they tell you that they are perfect since everybody has flaws. All you can do is believe in yourself and tell the voice inside your head to shut up. This book will help you learn how to shut the inner voice and believe in yourself.

Thank you once again for purchasing the book. I hope it helps you.

Chapter One: Negative Self-Talk and How it Affects You

Everybody has an inner critic that helps to motivate to achieve his or her goals. This critic helps you stick to a diet or lifestyle depending on what your goal is. However, if you do not check this voice, it will harm you, particularly if you are negative about life. This voice is called negative self-talk and it can bring you down before you realize what has happened to you.

Most people experience negative self-talk at least once in their lives, and this talk comes in multiple forms. You can also be under stress because of this talk thereby affecting the people around you if you are not careful. This chapter provides information on what negative self-talk is and how it affects your mind, body, life and your relationships.

What is Negative Self-Talk

Negative self-talk takes a variety of forms. For instance, it can help you stay grounded by telling you that there are somethings you must avoid to stay safe and healthy. There are times when it can sound mean by telling you that you can never do anything right. You can also use this voice to take a realistic approach or develop fear or a fantasy.

The musings or thoughts of your inner critic can sound like a critical friend or partner from the past. This voice can take the path of cognitive distortions like blaming and catastrophizing. In other words, negative self-talk is that voice inside you that limits your ability and prevents you from believing in yourself. These thoughts diminish your ability to change your life. Negative self-talk isn't just stressful, but it can also hinder your success.

How to Spot Negative Thinking

Let us look at some of the common forms of negative self-talk.

Filtering

Regardless of what the situation is, you will focus on the negative aspects of the situation and ignore the positive ones. For instance, let us say that you had a great day of work. You completed every task assigned to you on time and did a thorough job of it. People showered you with compliments. However, you forget about those compliments and only focus on the tasks that you were unable to complete. You then begin to work on more tasks and put yourself under stress.

Personalizing

When you are in a bad situation, you blame yourself regardless of whether you were at fault or not. For instance, if you hear that your friends cancelled on a night out, you will assume that nobody wanted to come because they did not want to be with you.

Catastrophizing

You always anticipate the worst in a situation. When you wake up and stub your toe, you tell yourself that you woke up on the wrong side of the bed. You convince yourself that you will have a horrible day.

Polarizing

Things or situations can only be good or bad. You never see the middle ground. Therefore, you strive to be perfect to ensure that every situation you are in is good. If there is ever a time when a situation is not in your favor, you convince yourself that you are a failure.

Toll of Negative Self-Talk

Negative self-talk has a disastrous effect on you. There are studies that link negative self-talk with low self-esteem and high levels of stress. This talk can lead to feelings of helplessness and demotivation. Therefore, it is important that you learn to fix this negative self-talk.

People who frequently engage in negative self-talk are often more stressed. This happens since their reality is slightly altered to help them experience the success they believe they have achieved. They need to create this experience since they do not see the many opportunities around them, and they do not capitalize on those opportunities. Therefore, the perception of stress is because of the change in behavior and perception. The consequences of the inner critic are listed below:

Limited Thinking

You constantly tell yourself that you cannot do something. The more you tell yourself that, you start to believe it. For example, if you tell yourself that you cannot pass an exam, you will start to believe it and eventually you will not pass that exam.

Perfectionism

You start to believe that you cannot just be great. You must be perfect and that you can attain that level of perfection. However, people who are high achievers often perform better than people who want to be perfectionists. This is because the former group of people are happier and less stressed when they do a job well. The latter often pick a task apart and see what they can do better next time.

Depressive Feelings and Emotions

Negative self-talk often leads to depressive feelings and emotions. This inner voice can lead to grave consequences if you do not check it early in life. For example, when you constantly tell yourself that you have no friends, you will start to feel depressed.

Challenges in Relationships

Negative self-talk changes the way you perceive yourself and others. It can turn you into an insecure and needy person. But, it makes you want to constantly criticize the people around you. It is because of this criticism that people will want to stay away from you.

An obvious drawback of negative self-talk is that it is not positive. It sounds simple, but research has shown that when you motivate yourself, you will succeed. For instance, a study was conducted on athletes where four types of self-talk were compared. It was found that positive self-talk helped an athlete succeed since they did not have to constantly remind themselves that they were doing great.

Chapter Two: How to Silence the Negative Talk

It is good to criticize yourself since it helps you become a better person. But, there is a great difference between telling yourself that you are a huge person and telling yourself that you should work out.

You should remember that your inner voice defines what success and failure is to you. When you criticize yourself excessively, it will backfire since you will focus more on failure. Instead of focusing on what you should have done better or what you should improve, you worry about the significance of the mistake. As mentioned earlier, negative self-talk is associated with depression and stress. This chapter gives you tips on how to stuff the muzzle of your inner critic.

Set Aside All the Negativity

When you beat yourself up, you inflate a small mistake into a huge failure. When you begin to think negatively, take a few deep breaths. Once you are calm, break the problem down into segments and identify a solution to the smaller problems. Try to change the way you perceive a mistake. For example, if you made a mistake during a meeting, instead of telling yourself that you screwed up, you can tell yourself that you made a mistake and should find a way to make up for that mistake. It helps if you can set aside the negative and visualize a positive environment. When you see that the problem fits into the smallest box possible, you will develop confidence.

Possible Thinking

People will always ask you to think positively when you are upset. However, research has found that saying positive things to yourself when you are upset only makes you feel worse. This is because your brain defines these positive thoughts as lies. Experts suggest that you use a technique called possible thinking where you only reach for neutral thoughts about a situation. For example, "I am huge." becomes "I need to lose weight, and I know exactly how to do it." When you focus on the facts, you can choose which path you want to take.

Stop Questioning Yourself

Let us assume that you were in a meeting and you blurted out that your bra was too tight. You tell yourself that you have made a fool of yourself. But, think about the situation – was everybody in the meeting paying attention to you or were they busy tapping on their phones?

One of the best ways to be kind to yourself is by questioning your thoughts. When you ask yourself more questions, you will feel better about some situations and not worry about what someone has to say about you. For example, instead of asking yourself, "How could I have been so stupid to say that in front of everybody?" tell yourself that you made a mistake and it is okay.

Change Your Outlook

Change the way you look at situations. Instead of telling yourself, "I cannot do this today. Serves me right for being disorganized." tell yourself, "I am not sure I can do this today."

This may seem silly, but a change in wording gives you the feeling that this moment is just a moment. When you tell yourself that you are stupid, you define who you are. However, when you say that you felt stupid, you convince yourself that you are not stupid, but only felt stupid in that moment.

Be Your Own Friend

When you make mistakes at work or in life, the first person you will share this mistake with is your friend. How does your friend react when you tell him or her something – "Are you sure it was that bad that it will ruin your career?"

Another thing to remember is that you should never tell yourself what you would not tell your friend. You know that you will never call your friend a slob if he or she drops food on his clothing. So, why should you call yourself one?

Name Your Critic

Give your inner critic a silly name. It is difficult to take your critic seriously when you address it with a funny name. For example, Brene Brown, a professor at the University of Houston Graduate College of Social Work refers to her inner critic as the Gremlin! When you name the inner critic something funny, it will break the emotional hold that the voice has over you. This will in turn help you break the anxiety cycle.

Name Your Rants too

Some psychologists call these inner thoughts and rants stories. You can name every thought that passes through your mind and every memory you have ever made. When you take a step back and go through all the stories, you will realize that the premise to most stories is the same. The same thoughts pass through your mind regularly, which should help you understand that these are not thoughts but habits. These habits are not the truth.

Pick Up the Phone

You only feel shame when you keep everything a secret. For example, if you went to a party and did something stupid, leave the place and call your friend. When you tell him or her what transpired at the party, he or she will laugh. At that moment, you will have cut off shame at the knees. Find the courage to speak to someone and laugh at yourself at what you did.

Embrace Your Flaws

It is important that you stop holding yourself to high standards. It is destructive to be a perfectionist. If you read an interview given by the CEO of a company, you will never hear them tell you that they are perfect. Instead, they credit their success to a mistake they made. They tell about what they learned from the mistake they made and how it shaped their goal.

Relax your standards a little and show yourself some empathy. You can win over the Nag with ease!

Chapter Three: Positive Thinking

How do you answer this question – is your glass half-full or half-empty? I am sure you may have come across this question earlier. The answer to this question defines how you look at life and your attitude towards yourself. The answer to this question also affects your mental health.

Many studies have concluded that traits like pessimism and optimism affect many areas of your physical and mental wellbeing. When you are optimistic, you have a positive outlook on life. Therefore, you can manage your stress with ease thereby improving your mental wellbeing. If you are pessimistic and listen to your inner critic, do not fret. You can develop positive thinking skills.

Understand Positive Self-Talk and Positive Thinking

When someone says positive thinking, it does not necessarily mean that you should ignore the less pleasant situations in your life. When you think positively, you can approach an unpleasant situation in a productive and positive way. You begin to believe that the bets will happen to you and not the worst.

Positive thinking starts with positive self-talk. You can transform all the stream of negative self-talk into positive talk using the tips mentioned in the previous chapter. Often, self-talk comes from reason and logic, but there are times when this talk arises from misconceptions that you create because you lack information.

Benefits of Positive Thinking

Experts continue to study the benefits of positive thinking on physical and mental health. Some benefits include:

- Lower levels of depression

- Increased life span

- Resistance to diseases like the common cold

- Lower levels of distress

- Better physical and psychological well-being

- Reduced risk of cardiovascular diseases

- Better heart health

- Better coping mechanisms during times of stress and hardship

Researchers must conduct further studies to understand how positive thinking benefits health. A theory is that when you think positively you can deal with stressful situations better. This reduces the effects that stress has on your body. People with a positive approach towards life lead healthier lifestyles since they follow a healthy diet, get more physical activity and do not drink or smoke in excess.

How to Focus on Positive Thinking

You can turn your negative thoughts into positive thoughts with ease. It is a simple process, but it takes practice and time. This is because you are developing a new habit. This section gives you some tips that you can use to start thinking positively.

Identify the Areas to Change
Before you begin to think positively, you should identify the areas in your life where you always think negatively. These areas can be work, relationships, your travel or education. You must start small and focus on one area. Try to approach any situation in that area positively before you move on to another area.

Check Yourself
Always stop and evaluate your thoughts at some point during the day. If you find that you only have negative thoughts, identify a way to add some positivity to those thoughts.

Be Open to Humor
You must laugh or smile when you are in a difficult situation. Try to look for humor in every situation. If you can laugh when you are stressed, you will feel better and can take the world on with renewed energy.

Follow a Healthy Lifestyle

Exercise for at least 30 minutes every day on four or five days of the week. You can break the time up into ten-minute intervals and exercise any time during the day. Exercise is an activity that has a positive affect on your mood and helps to reduce stress. Follow a healthy diet to ensure that you have enough energy throughout the day.

Surround Yourself with Positive People

You must ensure that the people in your life are supportive, positive and you can depend on them when you are under stress. These people should be willing to give you advice when needed and give you constructive feedback when necessary. Negative people increase your stress levels and make you doubt your capabilities.

Practice Positive Self-Talk

As mentioned earlier, you should follow a simple rule – never tell yourself something you will not say to another person. Always be gentle with yourself and encourage yourself to do better. If you start to think negatively, evaluate the situation, and tell yourself what it good about you. Think about the things in your life that you are grateful for.

How to Practice Positive Thinking Every day

When you feel negativity in life, you cannot expect to turn into an optimist overnight. However, with practice your inner critic will become more of a friend. You will accept yourself for who you are and take your tasks up with renewed enthusiasm. When your state of mind is optimistic, you can handle stress in a constructive way. This is an ability that only those who think positively possess.

Chapter Four: Exercises to Remove Negative Self-Talk

Your reality is created by what you think and every thought you have is developed based on the beliefs you hold in your mind. When you are aware of what is happening in your mind and you take control of it, you change your innate beliefs and thoughts that are responsible for making you who you are.

The previous chapters talked about what negative self-talk are and how you can silence your inner voice. This chapter leaves you with some exercises that will help you deal with negative thoughts. You can perform these exercises when you are aware that you are thinking negatively.

You may have told yourself that you will practice these exercises regularly because you are willing to change the way you think. However, you may lead a busy schedule, and therefore, it becomes difficult for you to perform these exercises. Therefore, it is important that you set a reminder every day. Set aside some time every morning or night to perform these exercises.

Track your progress by using either sticky notes or journals. You can also use them to remind you about the activities that you must perform. Stick these notes in your bathroom, bedroom, kitchen and every other place in your house that you visit frequently, to remind you that it is time to perform the exercise. It may seem unnecessary to remind yourself in every possible way, but it is essential since you are changing the way you talk to yourself. Let us look at some exercises that you can perform regularly to change the way you think.

Ho'oponopono Process

The Ho'oponopono Process is an ancient Hawaiian healing process that works on your energy. This exercise has helped many people remove negative thoughts and foster positive thinking. When you perform this exercise, you not only alter your external reality, but also change your body. This is because the process works only on your energy and uses that energy to heal you. You should look at some of the different explanations available on the Internet to help you understand the process better. You can learn more about the process in the following article: The Updated Ho'oponopono and Dr. Joe Vitale's Zero Limits.

Affirmations

It is obvious that positive affirmations are a great way to start thinking positively. Depending on what your needs are, you can choose any positive affirmation and repeat that throughout the day. With affirmations, you can change your negative thoughts into positive thoughts. This means that you should keep your thoughts in check and immediately use a positive affirmation which will lift you up and help you change the belief that is giving you this thought. Through affirmations, you can identify the beliefs that make you think negatively. You can replace or remove those beliefs with positive affirmations and beliefs. Affirmations work since they work on the principles of the law of attraction. You attract what you believe.

Short Stories

In this method, you can tell yourself a short story that you have written which brings some happy and positive images to your mind. You can use this method when you feel low or are having a bad day. You can use this method in two ways:

- Like the previous method, when you find yourself thinking negatively about a situation, stop yourself. Instead of using affirming thoughts, you can tell yourself a story of how the future can look for you. You can also tell yourself about your hopes and dreams. When you are good at this, you will stop worrying yourself with negative thoughts and create a better space for yourself. You will learn to expect that only good things will happen.

- The second method is like the first, except for the fact that you will tell yourself a story that is not related to the negative thought. You cannot expect to always think positively because it is not something that is good for the mind. Therefore, it is best to avoid negative thoughts in any situation and replace them with a story about an unrelated topic. To do this, you should tell yourself a story of your possible future that is related to any other aspect of your life.

Good Memories

One of the most common things about life is that we are never in the same place in our lives every step of the way. There is something that constantly changes in our lives. You can deny this, but there is always a small or big change in life. You may be better at a task or things may have taken a turn for the worse.

It can be that you are not doing well in a specific area in your life, and this part of your life was better at some point. Things may not have been great then, but it never bothered you. So, all you need to do in this situation is tell yourself about an event that happened in the past where things were always right. This will help to control any negative emotion you may have about the situation.

Your friends will often remind you about the good times. Even Facebook reminds you about a memory of yours from four years ago. Cherish those memories. You do not have to become the person you were a few years ago. All you must do is realize that this moment is precious and it will be a memory in the distant future.

Regardless of how you feel, it is important to talk to yourself about some moment in your past that left an impression on you. This memory will help you change your mindset.

Conclusion

Everybody goes through a phase in life when they think negatively about how the situation is. However, if most of the thoughts that run in your mind are negative, you will only have a pessimistic outlook on your life. These negative thoughts stem from your inner beliefs. Your inner critic voices these beliefs out and tells you that you are not good at doing anything. It is important that you remove these negative thoughts to ensure that you lead a happy life.

Over the course of the book, you will gather information on what negative self-talk is and how you can identify it. You will also learn how to silence this voice and focus more on the positive aspects of life. There are some exercises in the book that will help you change your beliefs and thoughts. Practice these exercises regularly to ensure that you lead a happy life.

I wish you luck on your journey.

Social Skills

Top 10 Mistakes That Destroy Your Charisma... and How to Avoid Them

By

Stuart Killan

Introduction

I want to thank you for choosing this book, *'Shyness: Top 10 Mistakes That Destroy Your Charisma...and How to Avoid them'* and hope you find it informative.

Over the course of the book, you will gather information on what charisma is and the qualities that a charismatic person possesses. You will also gather information on what you should not do to destroy your charisma. It is important to remember that when one loses faith in you, it is hard to obtain that same level of trust. I hope the information in the book helps you stick to your beliefs and redefine yourself as a person.

Marilyn Monroe proved that one does not have to have an air about them to be charismatic. She was walking with a photographer and magazine editor towards the Grand Central Terminus deep in conversation. It was a busy day and the terminus was packed with people, and nobody had the time to look at her. As the photographer clicked the camera, she boarded the train and sat in the corner of a car.

Marilyn wanted to show the magazine editor that she could either choose to be plain Norma Jean Baker or glamorous Marilyn Monroe just by deciding. She was Norma Jean on the subway, but when she reached the sidewalks of New York, she chose to be Marilyn. She turned to the photographer and asked him if he would like to see Marilyn. All she did was turn around, fluff her hair and strike a pose, and she turned into the glamorous Marilyn Monroe.

A spark rippled out of her and she became magnetic. The people walking past her stopped in their tracks and recognized that a star was in their midst. In an instant, fans engulfed Marilyn and it took some time for the photographer to protect her from the crowd.

Charisma is a controversial and intriguing topic. People believe that charisma is a characteristic that people either have or do not have. There are some people who believe that charisma is often taken advantage of, while there are others who want to learn it. Regardless of how they feel about charisma, people are fascinated by it. Charismatic people have a significant impact on the world.

Have you ever wondered what it would be like to be as charismatic as Steve Jobs or Bill Clinton? Everybody has some charisma, but they can destroy it easily. Over the course of this book, you will gather information on what charisma is, and how people tend to destroy it. You will also learn what you should do to ensure that your actions do not destroy your charisma.

Stuart Killan

I hope you gather all the information that you are looking for.

Chapter One: What is Charisma?

People often struggle when they must define the word charisma. They find it especially hard to define the word in relation to social sciences and communication. Charisma is ultimately the result of good interpersonal and communication skills. Since one can learn to develop these skills, one can also learn to be charismatic.

How to be Charismatic

To become charismatic, you should pay attention to how you interact with people. A charismatic person has some qualities that appeal to others, and these qualities are all positive traits. They use their skills to attract people to them, and know what to say to ensure that people agree with them regardless of what the discussion is. It is for this reason that charisma is closely related to leadership skills, and it is important for a successful leader to be charismatic. Both Barack Obama and Bill Clinton are charismatic, and so are their wives. Their charisma helped them achieve success.

If someone asks you to think of a charismatic person, you will not think about yourself. You will first think about a celebrity, successful leader or a politician. It is true that their charisma led them to be successful, but there are many ordinary people who are charismatic. The staff at the restaurant making the most tips, the cool girl in school, the popular person in the office and the girl everybody wants to know, all have one thing in common – they are charismatic.

There are some people who are more charismatic when compared to others but, what makes you realize that someone is charismatic? Let us look at some of the characteristics of a charismatic person. Remember that you can develop these traits with ease.

Traits of a Charismatic Person

Self-Confidence

Charismatic people know how to appear confident, or are confident people. It is hard for most people to communicate or voice out their opinion when they are in a meeting, in a group, or speaking to an audience. A charismatic person knows how to communicate with people and helps other people also feel confident. This helps to enhance the process of communication. A charismatic person does not boast and is not egotistical. He or she is only confident about his values and beliefs.

Being Optimistic

Since a charismatic person is confident, he or she appears to also be optimistic. This means that they always try to see the best in a situation, event or in a person. They are often bubbly and cheery, and encourage people to be the best version of themselves. This helps people around them to have a positive outlook towards life.

An Emotional Player

To appear optimistic and confident, a person must act. Charismatic people can show their true emotions when they realize that their acting works in their favor. They also learn to mask their emotions and beliefs if they need someone to follow or agree with their beliefs. A charismatic player is like a swimming swan. He or she appears serene and calm on the surface, but there is a lot of internal activity that they hide from the public.

Being Interested and Interesting

Charismatic people know when they should listen to someone and when they want people to listen to them. They are good storytellers and know how to engage the crowd. They often communicate their messages concisely and clearly, and know when to be serious and when to inject humor in their conversation. They also know when to engage the audience, and how to ensure that the audience focuses on their speech.

Charismatic people know how to pay attention to the audience and will observe them to see what they can do better. If they are speaking to a small group or one person, they use relaxed and open body language while making eye contact. If they address a large group, they try to use their body language to let the audience know that they want to include everybody in the discussion.

They are often interested in others and ask questions to understand the opinions, feelings and views of other people. They do not have to extract information from people because they know how to make people feel at ease. People do not lie to them because they trust them to be open and honest. A charismatic person can sympathize and empathize with the people he or she speaks to and tries to remember details from previous conversations. This helps them build trust.

Maintaining eye contact, a simple smile, being courteous and polite are effective ways of making people understand your point. If you treat people well, they will be willing to do things for you.

Demonstrating and Being Intelligent

Since charismatic people want to communicate with people effectively, they know how to initiate a conversation with others. They often read and have sound knowledge about the current affairs and general knowledge. It makes it easier for them to make small talk with some people and move past the awkward beginning of the conversation.

Charismatic people are experts in some fields and know how to break complex concepts down in a way that helps their audience understand the concept. They also know how to change the explanation according to how the audience is receiving the information. This knowledge makes people trust charismatic people.

Being Assertive

Charismatic people know how to unite people over a common cause, or make them believe what they want them to. Most people use this ability for good causes, but there are others who use it to assert their right over others. Charismatic leaders can influence their followers and motivate people to do what they want. Some con artists are charismatic and they use their skills to gain respect and trust from their victims, and then they extort valuables and money from their victims.

It is hard to identify if a charismatic person is assertive since they are very subtle about it. They know what they should say to persuade people with words and emotions. They use their ability to understand their emotions and the emotions of the people around them, and use that knowledge to assert their beliefs.

Maintaining Attention to Detail

Charisma is about attention to detail. It also depends on interpersonal interactions. To be charismatic, you must learn to communicate effectively with enthusiasm and passion, while you display positive body language. You must think positively, be optimistic and display self-confidence. Charisma is also about building respect and about being persuasive whenever necessary.

You can be more charismatic by working on your interpersonal skills through practice. It is important to remember that you cannot please people all the time, regardless of how charismatic you are.

Chapter Two: How do People Destroy their Charisma?

When people work hard on their interpersonal skills, they become charismatic; however, some people destroy their charisma by being too mean or too proud of themselves. This chapter lists out the ten mistakes that people often make that destroy their charisma.

Never Introducing Themselves

Some people barge in on conversations and voice out their opinion. They forget that they should introduce themselves first and ask for permission to speak since they are not leading the discussion. For example, you can say, "Hi, I apologize for intruding, but I would like to introduce myself." That way, people know that you are polite and will include you in the conversation.

There are times when people are too shy and avoid making eye contact with the people they are speaking to. When you do not look someone in the eye when you speak to them, you have lost them. They will not pay attention to you because they know you are not confident about what you are saying, and they will look for a way to get out of the conversation.

Not Introducing Your Friends or Guests

If you bring a friend to a party, you should ensure that you introduce that friend to the people at the party. Ensure that you do not shut your friends out. If you do not treat your inner circle well, you come across as being conceited and that you do not care for others. For example, if you are conversing with a group of friends, include your guests in the conversation by asking them what they think. If you do not make people feel welcome, they will stop hanging out with you.

Talking about Things that People do not Care About

You may love watching Anime or Sports, but some people may like to do the same thing. You can talk to them about it, but if you drone on and on about the same thing, boredom kicks in and people will want to leave the conversation.

You can tell people that you had a bad day at work, but if you give them every detail about your day, they will stop listening to you. You should ensure that you make the people around you comfortable and listen to what they have to say too. They should not leave the conversation with the impression that they wasted their time by listening to what you had to say about your life.

If you are running out of conversation starters, you can use some of the topics mentioned in the book, '*Shyness: 66 Easy Conversation Topics You Can Use to Talk to ANYONE.*'

Never Taking Feedback

You must pay attention to the audience and see how they react to a specific topic. When you see that people have not reacted to something you have said, you should stop and ask them a question to understand their views better. If the conversation does not shift back to what you were initially saying, you should take a hint and not go back to that topic. There is a possibility that people were zoning you out. When you do not take feedback into account, you show the people around you that their opinions do not matter. This turns people off and they may never want to speak with you again. You should also give feedback when someone else is talking.

Judging Others

It is not enough to have the confidence to show people your true personality. You should also learn to accept people for who they are. You cannot judge someone regardless of where they live, their occupation or where they come from. You must never let prejudice control your emotions. If you have read 'Pride and Prejudice,' you will remember that Elizabeth rejected Darcy's advances because she knew that he condemned others for being who they were. He also judged their circumstances. This is not the type of person you want to be.

Mumbling

A charismatic person exudes confidence. He or she knows what they are saying and knows how to convince people that they are right. If you begin to mumble or constantly stutter, people will lose interest in your conversation. You must ensure that you are loud and confident about whatever you are saying. You need to keep the people engaged and hooked to your conversation.

Giving One-Word Answers

Never give people one-word answers because they ask you a question to understand your opinion. If they ask you a question about the weather, you do not have to give them an elaborate answer about how you feel but, if they ask you about something on the news or about a holiday, do not give them one-word answers. You should try to elaborate and explain to them why you feel a specific way. When answering about the holiday, you can tell them about what you did and the places you visited.

Whining or Complaining

It is true that life is not as easy as people make it out to be. Even the most successful people have trouble in life but, do they whine? Do you think you can sort the problem out if you constantly whine or complain about how life is for you? You can mention that there is an issue that is troubling you, but you cannot talk about it constantly. Nobody likes people who complain, and I am sure you do not like them too. If you constantly complain to another person, you are being a hypocrite.

As Bob Marley said, "When you worry, you make it double." Many studies concluded that people who often complained were lazy. They also took it upon themselves to bring their friends down with them. It is important to remember that there is nothing more unattractive than a person who does not want to do well in life.

Never Remembering Names

When you are talking to someone, you should remember his or her name. You can use the Dale Carnegie method and repeat their name back to them. If you still do not remember their name, you can ask them to spell it out for you. It is rude to forget someone's name and expect them to listen to your conversation. You should avoid repeating their name constantly because that is a sign of submission.

Lacking Ideas and Principles

Everybody has insecurities because there is massive pressure to fit in. People often hide their true beliefs and principles because they worry that those beliefs will brand them as being weird but, when you lack principle, people will not remember you. Can you name any public figure who has no principles? I bet you cannot name even one. These principles do not always have to be right.

You must ensure that you are always true to yourself and do not succumb to others' expectations of you. People who stand out are given respect because they stick to their character regardless of what the situation may be.

Chapter Three: How to Improve Charisma

We often forget to live in the present and worry about what the future will look like for us. This can affect us in many ways, and one of the effects of not living in the present is that you lose your charisma. If you partially listen to what someone says or ignore them, you cannot charm them.

There are many tips that you can use to improve charisma, but the most important thing you must do is focus on your mental state. You must improve the connection between your mind and body. This chapter provides three exercises that you can use to improve that connection. You will find that you can have great conversations within no time.

Always be Present in Any Conversation

Human beings hate uncertainty. Multiple surveys show that human beings will prefer to hear bad news than not know what the outcome of a situation is. Go back to a time when you were head over heels in love with someone. How did you feel when that person stopped responding to your calls and messages? You thought it was over, but you did not know for sure. So, what did you do? You held onto that uncertainty for days, weeks and months. People will notice the change in your behavior. This change will affect your other relationships too. When you are uncertain, you often stop focusing on the present.

To fix this, you must note when your thoughts begin to wander when you are talking to someone. You may think that the other person will not notice, but you are wrong on most occasions. Your expressions will let the person know that you have phased out of the conversation, and you cannot answer a question if he or she wants to know what you think. This will ruin your charisma.

When you notice that your mind has started to wander, you should start to focus on your breathing. When your mind comes back, pay attention to what the person is talking about. Another technique that you can use is to focus on how your toes feel. You can pull your mind back and make it focus on one spot. This will make it easier for you to shift to the current conversation.

Lighten Your Load

When you are highly stressed, it will affect your social skills. There are some people who enjoy telling others how busy they are and talk about what a rush they are in. This will buy them attention for a small period, but the people who remain calm and cool are the ones who win the battle. You must remember that people love it when another person makes them feel at ease.

To bring yourself to this state, perform the following exercise before you meet someone:

- Take five minutes and sit down in a calm spot in your house.

- Imagine the issues that are stressing you out.

- Now, visualize that you have given up on these tasks and asked somebody else to take care of them temporarily. It can be your friend, colleague or even the Universe. This may sound easy, but it is hard to do.

When you perform this exercise, you will feel better and will find that you can participate in conversations freely. You will also encourage the people around you to let their guard down.

Make them Feel Like a Star

Most amateurs know what it takes to look smart but, people who have exceptional interpersonal and social skills know how they can make other people the star of the conversation. When you talk to someone, you should avoid bragging about yourself, because that comes off as trying too hard to make an impression. This is when the other person knows you are insecure about who you are. Instead of focusing on yourself, ask the other person about them and make them feel good about themselves.

You can only be this way if you have practiced. You must strike the right balance between being charming and sucking up to someone. When you identify the right mix, people will want to be with you. You can become a dynamic speaker and work with people around you in a way you never have before. Remember that you are successful when you can make the people around you feel good about themselves.

Other Tips

Use Metaphors

You can use metaphors when you talk about your group. This group can be a sports team or an army. Lady Gaga refers to her fans as "Little Monsters." When Prince slapped the word "slave" across his face and appeared on television, he invoked a very powerful metaphor. Charismatic people use metaphors since it helps them stir a person's imagination and emotions.

Use Anecdotes and Stories

It is important to use stories and anecdotes when you talk about your successes and failures. You can tell people a story of how you failed and what you did to overcome that failure. Many rock stars use these failures to establish a connection with their audience and their music. For example, Paul McCartney always started off with an anecdote when he sang a song he had written about someone. He would tell the audience a little story about the person before he performed.

Moral Conviction

As mentioned earlier, it is important that you stick to your beliefs and opinions. When you are confident about your beliefs, you appeal to people. When you tell people that they have to do the right thing, you indicate to them that you stick to your values. Many rock stars displayed moral conviction, and this helped them strengthen their bond with the audience. U2 had their fans marching around the stage when Aung San Suu was arrested. To support the Russian group that was imprisoned, Madonna printed the words "Pussy Riot" on her back.

Express Shared Feelings

If you feel the same way as another person, you should express that emotion. This expression helps to increase and strengthen the bond between the two of you. When you say, "I am excited about this opportunity," or "I am as overwhelmed as you are," you strengthen your connection.

Make Your Presence Known

You must let the people in the room know that you have arrived. You can only do this if you know how to carry yourself. When you watched Barack Obama give his speeches, you saw how the crowd kept quiet the minute he stepped onto the stage. This should be you if you want to be charismatic. The people you speak to should give you their time and listen to you. They should not interrupt you; however, these people should not be afraid of you. You should also give them the freedom to voice out their opinion and stick to their beliefs whenever necessary. People do not like the idea of a "Yes" man.

You can practice your walk, your gestures and your body language, before you enter a room. This will help you maintain your cool and help you grasp the attention of the crowd.

Conclusion

Thank you for purchasing this book.

Charismatic people can grasp the attention of the people in the room when they enter the room or start talking. They can change the way people view them and build stronger relationships with people. Using their charm and wit, they can ensure that people trust their decisions and opinions. They do not use their charm or their power to make people do the wrong thing.

However, there are some people who lose their charisma or destroy it because they start to behave differently. For instance, too much stress can make people worry or wonder about what their day will look like tomorrow. What they forget is that people do not like it if others ignore them. It is small gestures like these that affect your charisma.

Conversation

66 Easy Conversation Topics You Can Use to Talk to ANYONE

By

Stuart Killan

Introduction

I want to thank you for purchasing this book, 'Shyness: 66 Easy Conversation Topics You Can Use to Talk to ANYONE.'

People often enjoy social gatherings where they can have a good time chatting with friends and acquaintances, eating and drinking. You may be talking to a large group of people or a single person, but you notice that the conversation is slowly dying. There is a possibility that you have only been talking about yourself, and have run out of things to say. It is important to remember that you when you converse with people, you should also give them a chance to speak.

So, how do you ensure that the conversation builds around a topic? Is there a way to ensure that the conversation does not die quickly? Can you say something to help the person feel at ease about conversing with you? You will find the answers to all those questions in this book.

Over the course of this book, you will gather information on what conversation threading is, and how you can use it to maintain a conversation with people, but how do you approach someone for the first time and start a conversation? What can you say that does not sound offensive or intrusive? There are some questions listed out in the book that will help you start a conversation with a person or a group of people you have just met. You can also make the conversations interesting by asking funny and weird questions.

I hope you like the questions in the book and use them to start conversations.

Chapter One: What is Conversation Threading?

It is easy to speak to people of all ages if you can thread conversations. You can turn a boring conversation into an interesting one if you know how to thread conversations. It is a simple technique where you use a word or a sentence and spin that into the premise of the conversation. You must ensure that the content of the new conversation is in sync with the conversation you had earlier. This may seem slightly abstract, so let us look at the following example. Let us assume that you ran into an acquaintance at the store.

You: "What did you do today?"

Acquaintance: "Thank you for asking. I had a pretty calm night – chilled out, drank a few beers, ordered in and watched some TV."

That answer did not give you something you can use to build into a conversation. This is where the technique of conversation threading comes into play. You should make note of the significant words in the answer – calm, chilled out, beers and television – and use those words to build a conversation. You can select the word that appeals to you, and use that word to build a conversation. The new conversation can be based on a similar topic, or can branch out into a different topic but, to make the conversation work, you must use the words from the previous conversation. Otherwise, the new conversation will be out of context.

Here are a few examples:

- Calm: "Ah, I am jealous. I wanted to have a calm night, but my friends came home and dragged me to a bar. It was a fun evening though."

- Beer: "Oh, I love beer; however, I prefer whiskey or scotch. It is funny though that my parents did not like the idea of me drinking when I was a teenager but, when I spoke to my mother last night and was complaining to them that I could not sleep, she asked me to drink a pint before bedtime. This was weird coming from my mother, but I took her advice and downed a beer, and, guess what, I slept like a baby."

How to Use Themes

I hope you got the picture here. The best thing about this technique is that with a little practice, you can do this for any theme. You can start conversations based on themes instead of words if the current theme shares the same premise as the prior conversation. For instance, if you use the answer above, you will find some themes like:

- Comfortable and stress-free

- Movie and entertainment

- Party, food and alcohol

You can use these themes to begin new conversations. Here are some examples:

Entertainment: "Ah! Yes, I love watching television too when I relax. I love watching TX series like Californiacation and Friends. Those are two of my favorite shows, and I think Hank Moody from Californiacation is one of the coolest TV characters – every guy wants to be like him and girls want to be with a man like him.

Alcohol: "Now that you mention it, I realize it has been quite some time since I had a drink. I stopped drinking a few weeks ago, because I am training to run a marathon. I also wanted to see what it would be like to avoid drinking and going out. It was hard, but I have started to enjoy staying at home and pursuing my hobbies."

Final Thoughts

Avoid flipping or changing the meaning of the themes or words from responses. For example:

Acquaintance: "I had a fantastic day today."

You: "Oh wow, I watched the Fantastic Four movie a few hours ago."

If you flip the meaning of the words or sentence, your reply will seem out of context, and that ruins the idea behind conversation threading. You should also avoid overdoing it. You do not have to necessarily use every word in the response to begin a new conversation. I did this earlier to help you understand how you can thread conversations. You can come across as unnatural if you pull out more than one word or theme from the answers.

Only use conversation threading as a tool when you are making conversation. Avoid overusing it. It is natural to spin the conversation using some keywords or themes, but a free-flowing conversation will not consist only of keywords or themes since the conversation will move from one theme to the next. If a conversation is going well, enjoy it and continue the conversation.

However, you do not have to spin conversations only once if you want to move away from a boring conversation. You can use these techniques to spin a conversation until you land on a topic that you like. Stay in that conversation until it begins to lose momentum. Ensure that you shift from one conversation to the other before it goes stale.

How to Implement Conversation Threading

You must always practice before you use a new technique when you converse with people. Practice conversation threading on friends and try to keep the conversation going. You can also practice with your partner. All you need to do is trade one sentence with your partner and use conversation threading to maintain the flow of the conversation. Do not ask questions.

Steering a Conversation

There are some people who always complain about their lives and constantly talk about negative stuff. You can use conversation threading to steer the conversation away from negativity. Ensure you don't do this because you don't want them to speak to you; you are doing this to build a connection with them.

Chapter Two: Conversation Starters to Break the Ice

It is hard to break the ice with someone you have met for the first time. Regardless of what event it is - a corporate event or a party - you do not have to hide in a corner. When you initiate a conversation with someone new, you may land an amazing opportunity, your next best friend or a potential date. If you are unsure of where to start, use the conversation starters listed below:

Tell me about Yourself

This is one of the classic conversation starters. You can ask the person to tell you something about the place he or she grew up in, something about their family (if they are willing to share that information with you) or about their childhood. This is a topic that puts people at ease since you are not asking them for personal information.

Do You have Pets?

People are always open to tell you about their pets. When you ask them questions about their pets, their face will light up and they will tell you anything you ask them about their pets. They may also be willing to share some pictures with you. If the person you are speaking to does not have pets, you can tell them about your pets. If you do not have pets, you can always tell them that you wish you had pets. Regardless of what the answer is, this topic is a good way to start making conversation.

Their Favorite Book

You should avoid asking someone what they are currently reading. This may sometimes be an intimate question; however, you can ask them if they are avid readers and ask them if they have read any of your favorite books. If they have, you can build a conversation around books and take it from there.

What they Do after Work

Ask them if they kick their shoes off and relax or hit the gym when they get home from work. Studies have shown that asking people how they relax, relaxes them.

Their Dream Job

A fun way to start a conversation is by asking someone what their dream job is. You can ask a person this question even if you are at a corporate gathering.

Their Favorite Cities or Countries

You can ask someone where they would like to live if they had the opportunity to live anywhere in the world. Only a few people travel as much as they would like to, which makes this an interesting way to start a conversation. You can also ask them if they travel frequently. You can ask them this question even if you do not travel since you are encouraging the person to share some of his or her memories.

Ask them if they Cook

If you want to continue to converse with the person, you can ask them if they cook. If they answer yes, you can ask them about them more about what they cook. You can also ask them about their favorite food and if they cook that food often. This is an icebreaker that works in any situation.

Their Favorite Drink

This is a basic question since you are only asking someone about a beverage that they love. It will work at any gathering since you can offer to bring them a glass of that beverage if it is available.

A Favorite Local Restaurant

This question gives people the chance to tell you about their favorite local spot. It puts everyone at ease since it gives them the chance to tell you about their favorite food in that restaurant.

Favorite Movie

People are always eager to tell you about their favorite movie. You can continue the conversation by asking them simple questions about the movie, the actors and the premise of the movie. You can also discuss the movie if you have watched it too.

The Movie they Want to Watch

This question can involve a large group of people. People will be eager to discuss the new releases, and talk about why they want to watch a specific movie.

Favorite TV Series

This is an open-ended question and does not offend anybody. Even the people who are really shy participate in the discussion.

Last Concert

You can learn more about a person's tastes in music by asking them this question. It is a good question to ask one or two people you are talking to.

The Craziest Thing they have Done

If a person is willing to make a great first impression, he or she will want to grab the attention of the people around them. You can ask them this question to lead the group into a fun conversation.

What Item do You Want to have with You if You are Stranded on a Desert Island?

Whatever the answer to this question, you can just ask them the reason why they said it and so on the conversation continues.

Favorite Season

This is an easy question for most people to answer since it is easy to talk to someone about the weather. You can follow up by asking them about the weather that day and build a conversation.

Languages

This is a semi-personal question since it encourages people to share some information about themselves with you.

Plans for the Weekend

It is easier to speak to someone about their future without giving them the vibe that you are stalking them. Try to keep the conversation fun and share your plans with them too.

That Dress is Lovely. Where did You Get it?

People love compliments, and appreciating someone's dressing sense is a good way to start a conversation. You can steer the topic easily towards fashion, aesthetics or simply the brand of clothing or shop from where they bought the dress.

Do You Know which Song is Playing?

Regardless of whether you know which song is playing or not, you can always ask someone to tell you about the music that is playing. It is a simple conversation starter.

How Long have You been Working for?

People either love their job or hate it, but they always have something to say about it. Use this question especially with those whom you have met at the work place. For others, use any other questions from the list.

What made You Laugh Today/this Week?

This question shows your interest in what makes the person laugh or happy, and can be a good icebreaker.

What will You do with a Million Dollars?

This is a direct question, but one that can make a good impression.

How are You Today?

This is a genuine and probably the easiest way to start a conversation. Remember to sound like you mean it when you ask this question.

What is Your Favorite Vacation Spot?

It is wonderful to take a vacation. When you ask someone about their favorite destination, you make them feel at ease. You can build the conversation by asking them to give you more information about their favorite destination, and tell them about your favorite destination.

Have You Read the News Today?

If there was something interesting in the newspaper that morning, you can bring that topic into the conversation. Try to stay away from religion and politics since most people are sensitive to those topics.

What is Your Story?

This question is a direct way to speak to someone, but it can also come off as a pick-up line.

Have You been Here Before?

If you are at a corporate gathering or a social event, you can compliment the venue and ask the person you are speaking to about the venue.

What Animal will You be, and Why?

You can use this question to break the ice. Some answers can leave the group in stitches.

Which Famous Person will You Invite for Dinner and Why?

People love to talk about personalities they love. Ask this and watch the conversation take an interesting turn.

What is Your Favorite Holiday?

The idea or talk of travel and holiday relaxes a person and they will happily be a part of the conversation.

What is the Craziest Food You have Eaten?

When you ask a group this question, they will begin to think about the weird food they have eaten. If you feel awkward when you join a group that is already talking, you can use this question to join the conversation.

What can You not Live Without?

There is no wrong answer to this question. It can be chocolate, wine, food, sleep, or bread, etc.

Have You Won Something?

You are happy when you win an event or a competition; therefore, it is a great idea to ask someone if they have won something. They will like to share some information with you about their special day.

Do You have Siblings?

This is a personal question, but people are willing to share some information with you about their family. It is a smart way to make a connection with the person you are speaking to.

Have You Met Someone Famous?

Everybody is excited and happy when they meet someone famous. This question helps you break the ice with someone you have just met since you can share your experiences.

What is Your Preferred Mode of Communication?

This is a good question to start a conversation. You can follow this question up by asking for their contact number or email ID.

Chapter Three: Funny and Weird Conversation Starters

1. What if Your Clones Populated the World?

Ask the people around you if they would like to see more of themselves every day. This will help you understand how much a person loves himself or herself.

2. What Old People Things do You do?

You can ask people if they run Matlock marathons or mow their garden regularly. Regardless of what the answer is, you will hear some embarrassed chuckles.

3. What was Cool when You were Younger, but is not Cool now?

This question will result in nostalgia, but is also mildly self-deprecating. You can think of all the trends that once were fascinating to you and are now ridiculous – flannel shirts, bell-bottoms, mullets, and ripped jeans, etc. There are a lot of conversation topics that can stem from this question.

4. If You had a Reality TV Show, What would it be About?

This question can lead to some amusing answers. Pick the answer that fascinated you the most, and build a conversation around that.

5. What would be Your Name if You were in a Witness Protection Program?

You can expect some weird answers to this question, but it also gives people the opportunity to think about how they would like to start their life over.

6. Which of the Seven Dwarfs do You Relate Most to?

Each of the seven dwarfs has a personality type, so indirectly you are asking them how they see themselves. You will get some interesting insight about the person here.

7. A Morning Person or a Night Owl

Some people rise at dawn and go for a run or study, while others like to catch up on a TV series or go out partying at night. You can build a conversation around their schedule and find out what they like to do best. Which candy bar will you like to be?

8. Which Candy Bar do You Like the Most?

Most people love candies, so there is a good chance you will get the other person talking about their favorite candy. In case if they don't like sweet, you can pose a question asking them about their favorite food or savory food item.

9. How Long do You Think You would Last in a Zombie Apocalypse?

People always imagine what it will be like to survive in one of the zombie movies, but do you know how long you would last? This question can open a fun and lively debate.

10. What is Your Weapon of Choice?

How will you defend yourself if zombies were chasing you? The answers can be interesting since some people may choose to use semi-automatics, but there are some who may want to use swords.

11. Do You Think You would Like a World with Magic in it?

How do you think the world would be if there was magic in it? You can ask people to imagine they were in a fantasy show or book while considering real consequences of having magic in the world.

12. What would You do with a Thousand Acres of Land?

People can either want to be farmers or cowboys. This question is a fun way to start a conversation if it is dying.

13. Do You Want to Hack into Someone's Computer? If Yes, Whose and Why?

This is a tricky question and many people will choose not to answer it. You should understand the people you are with before you ask them this question. Also, ensure that you know where you are – if you are at a corporate gathering, you do not want to ask people this question.

14. What would the Theme be if You Built a Hotel? What would the Rooms look Like?

This is another creative conversation starter and can allow people's imagination to go wild. The answers can reflect a person's passion or something bizarre about their imagination.

15. What would You rather not do – Watch a TV Series and Movies or Use Social Media?

This question will help you understand what the people around you prioritize.

16. Whom would You rather have Dinner with?

This can be an intrusive question, but it is a fun way to ask someone who they are interested in.

17. If You had an Extra $1,000, what would You Spend it on?

You can identify if a person has value for money through this question. You can also expect some funny answers that will improve the conversation.

18. If You could Master an Instrument on Earth, which Instrument would it be?

Music is one of the best conversation topics since you can break the ice and learn something about someone. This question can lead to the formation of a band or a simple jamming session.

19. What do You Prefer – a Live-In Chef or a Live-In Massage Therapist?

This question will give you an insight into what the people around you truly want.

20. Name a Movie You can Quote from Start to Finish?

You can use this question to find out which movie your friend, partner or any stranger will love to watch. This gives you the opportunity to have the perfect date or an amazing time with your friends.

21. If there is a Movie about Your Life, which Actor should Play You? Will I be in Your Movie?

You can learn more about how a person views himself. The answer will tell you who the person's favorite actor is.

22. If You had the Ability to Go Back in Time and Change Some Parts of Your Childhood, What would You Learn and Master Over the Years to Ensure that You would be an Expert Today?

You can find out what the person really wishes they could do. If they want to become a professional pianist, you can talk to them more about the composers they like and ask them if they would like to become a composer. This question leaves room for silly responses.

23. What Age would You Like to be for the Rest of Your Life?

Were your glory days between the ages of 20 and 25? Or beyond those years? This answer will help you understand how another person wants to live their life.

24. Do you Want an Easy Job Where You Work for Someone Else? Or, do You Want to Work Incredibly Hard for Yourself?

It is hard to strike a balance between independence and work; however, you can use this question to figure out what a person truly wants.

25. Would You Prefer to Live in Your Dream Home in an Expensive Area, or in a Sub-Par Location?

It is difficult to choose a place to live but, by asking this question, you understand a person's priorities and have fun considering the extremes.

26. Which is Worse as per You – Getting a Serious Bout of Cold or Getting Stuck in Bad Traffic?

This is just a basic question that tells you where the person stands vis a vis patience or sickness. It is basically like asking which one to choose between the devil and the deep blue sea.

27. Do You Want to Stand in Line, or do You Want to be the First Person to Get Your Order and Leave?

It is a hassle to wait regardless of where you are waiting, but this is a fun way to understand what bugs the person you are talking to.

28. If You were a Disney Character, Who would You be?

Disney characters are loved by all, young and old. Even if someone doesn't like these characters, they will have an opinion about these characters (could be good or bad), so you will have something to talk about.

29. Would You Accept a One-Way Ticket to Mars if it was Habitable?

This is a fun question since there is a sci-fi angle to it but, there is more to this question than meets the eye. You can understand if the person you are speaking to is adventurous.

Conclusion

Thank you once again for choosing this book.

It is important to know how to start a conversation with people, and how you should maintain that conversation. There are some people who do not know how to make conversation. They will tell you about their lives, but will never give you the opportunity to tell them about yourself. This is because they want to get their points across before they go speak to the next person. It is alright to want to put your point across, but it is a bad idea to never let the other person speak.

In this book, we learned how you can maintain a conversation for longer than ten minutes using the concept of conversation threading. It is difficult to converse with people you have just met and there is a possibility that the conversation will die quickly. To prevent that from happening, you can use the sixty-six questions listed in the book. Some of these questions will help you start a conversation with a stranger, and some will help you make the conversation interesting.

I hope you learn the art of conversation threading from the book.

Social Anxiety

7 Easy Ways to Overcome Your Inferiority Complex TODAY

By

Stuart Killan

Introduction

Thank you for purchasing this book, 'Social Anxiety: 7 Easy Ways to Overcome Your Inferiority Complex TODAY.'

Inferiority complex is why most people find it afraid to take chances since they feel unworthy. People with an inferiority complex are always negative, and this is a characteristic that develops since their childhood. They hide their pain and fear in their heart and mind. They find a way to develop some defense mechanisms to hide these insecurities, or build a wall around them that prevents others from seeing their weakness.

This book provides insights on what an inferiority complex is, and how it develops. You can also identify the signs of the development of an inferiority complex. These signs will help you check your responses to the situations that bring painful memories to your mind. There are some strategies you can use that will help you replace those memories with positive ones. You can also identify ways that will help you avoid being in such situations.

Over the course of this book, you will gather information on what the inferiority complex is, and how people develop that complex. There are some signs that people with an inferiority complex show. If you display any of the signs mentioned in this book, use the methods given in the last chapter to come out of feeling inferior to the people around you.

If you have some issues with self-esteem and often feel inferior, read on and you can have a more confident life!

Thank you for purchasing this book. I hope you enjoy it.

Chapter One: The Inferiority Complex

People often feel inferior at some point in their life. You may have felt inferior to a colleague, sibling or even a friend. It may have been a minor event for some people, but, for others, it can be the start of a major inferiority complex. This is a condition that begins during their childhood and manifests into every aspect of your life if you do not recognize the symptoms early in life. People who suffer from an inferiority complex are very sensitive and belittle themselves.

People with these limitations should identify, accept and overcome their limitations when they reach a certain age in life, but some constantly remember these limitations either due to peer pressure or because of an authoritative parent or adult. These limitations include emotional responses, cultural differences, physical appearances and some disabilities. These people exhibit some inferiority complex symptoms because of these reminders. To overcome the feelings of inferiority, they develop some defense mechanisms. They employ these mechanisms when people talk about their insecurities.

Difference between Feeling Inferior and the Inferiority Complex

You were inferior when you were a baby. You may scoff at this, but think about it. When you are a baby, you cannot stay alive on your own. You are fully dependent on an adult for your survival. As you grow up, adults who are stronger and more capable than you are surrounding you.

Alfred Adler, a famous psychologist, mentioned that it is a healthy motivation to feel inferior. When you see someone do better than you or receive constructive criticism, you will work hard to eliminate any weakness. When you do this, you motivate yourself to do better and feel more powerful; thereby removing any feeling of inferiority. When you feel inferior, you learn from the people around you; therefore, you work towards developing yourself and will eventually become a confident adult.

However, for some people, this feeling of inferiority overpowers them and it stops being useful or helpful. This is what psychologists call the inferiority complex. This complex paralyzes you and prevents you from doing things that you will be good at; thereby resulting in social anxiety or shyness. You may also begin to feel worthless and the fear of failure will prevent you from trying to do something in your life.

That is the difference between the inferiority complex and feeling inferior. When you feel inferior, you can improve the way you work and your life; however, if you have an inferiority complex, it means you feel incomplete and unworthy to work on tasks that you are good at performing. You also find it difficult to visualize that you will achieve something in the future.

Types of Inferiority

People follow a common pattern if they have an inferiority complex. Based on these patterns, people with an inferiority complex fall into two categories:

- People who know that they are good looking, successful and smart, and yet feel inferior. This feeling is mysterious because they believe they are not good enough, but do not know why they feel that way. If this is how you feel, the people around you will tell you, "You are so smart/successful/ beautiful/etc. I really do not know why you feel this way." The unfortunate thing is that you do not understand why you feel that way either; you just feel that way.

- People who know they are dumb, ugly, failures, boring, etc. and their flaws make it difficult for them to receive the friendship, affection and support from others. If you feel this way, you will learn to believe that you can solve any problem that you have if you were smart, good looking and successful, or whatever other reason you tell yourself. Here is a quick test – how would you complete the following sentence: "I will be confident, attractive and happy, if only I was _____."

Which category do you think you fall into? People in the first category feel that it is unrealistic that they are good at what they do. The people in the second category feel the way they do because they only focus on their flaws. Regardless of the category you fall in, you may have been stuck with this feeling for most of your life.

Chapter Two: Signs of an Inferiority Complex

Being Sensitive

If you are inferior, comments about your work or you will send you into a path of depression and self-hate for days or weeks. You feel miserable when someone rejects you or excludes you from any conversation. You want to stop caring about what someone says, but it is not that simple for you.

You may have read many articles on how to handle such comments. Most of these articles advise you to stop worrying about what someone says by giving you a rational argument. You may have come across multiple articles that tell you that another person's opinion about you does not matter. This advice does not help since it is difficult for people to reason their way out of feeling something that they did not force themselves into feeling in the first place.

The solution to stop being too sensitive to what people say about you is not to care less about their opinion. Instead, it is about caring more about what you think of yourself. People who do not care about what someone has to say about them only trust their values.

When your sense of judgment becomes stronger, you stop worrying about what someone has to say about you. This is important to learn, and it takes time for people to find their beliefs and stick to them. You may have heard people telling you that men or women who know who they are are very attractive. You may not have known what that meant. All they meant was that a person is attractive if he or she is firmly rooted to his or her core beliefs. This means that the person is not a pushover and only performs those actions and tasks that adhere to his beliefs.

Constantly Comparing Your Qualities

When you constantly compare your qualities with another person, you feel inferior or superior to them. This is an obvious fact. Let us take a closer look at the problem. Why do you believe that everybody is always more successful and better when compared to you? This is because you focus only on their best quality and compare yourself using that quality as the criterion.

You should remember that a person who is great at one thing is certainly going to be better than you at performing that task since he or she is good at it. For instance, if someone spends at least an hour at the gym, he or she is going to have a better body than you. If a classmate of yours tops every semester, it is because he or she works hard and prepares for the exam well.

You look at these people and tell yourself that you are worse than they are, and then feel inferior. Yes, it is true that you are not going to be as good as they are. This is because you are measuring your success and qualities against constantly changing criteria. You should remember that you could only be successful if you work hard in that area. This means that the people you are comparing yourself with probably neglect other areas of life.

You should always settle for being the best version of yourself. This will relieve you of your need to always meet another's standards. You are not superior or inferior, but are just you.

Submissive Behavior

There is a concept called social rank theory in psychology. This concept says that a person often acts the way he or she does and feels a specific way based on how they perceive their social rank or status to be. When you feel inferior to somebody, or think you have a low status when compared to others, you will begin to act submissive.

Most of the traits of a person who is shy are like that of someone who is submissive. Think of how people who are shy often act:

- Can never make eye contact

- Always talk softly

- Are afraid to assert their opinions

If a chimpanzee was to act this way, a scientist would label it as being submissive. This is where low confidence stems. Submissive people have an unconscious belief that stems from their core. They believe that people are superior, better and deserve more respect when compared to them. If you can overcome this feeling of insecurity, you will find it easier to be outgoing. A study conducted by Paul Gilbert explored the association between social anxiety, shame and depression using the social rank theory as the basis. The theory argues that a person's perception of social status and rank affects his or her mood and emotions. The results of this study confirmed that social anxiety, shame and depression are closely related to submissive behavior and the feeling of inferiority.

Perfectionism

Perfectionism and inferiority go together since they are rooted in comparison. If you are a perfectionist, you will never be happy with what you do. Let us consider the following scenario:

There was a boy named Joe who wanted to be an artist. He was a perfectionist and he believed that this quality would help him become the best artist there ever was; however, perfection doesn't make you best. Joe liked to visit online galleries and forums where he observed the work of some of the best artists across the globe. He believed that his work was terrible when compared to the work that they did. He felt that none of the work that he did would ever match up to the work that they did. He did not find the need to work any longer since his work will never be perfect. According to him, none of the famous artists in those galleries would appreciate his work. His comparison became unhealthy and he began to feel inferior to his competitors. He stopped painting because of this feeling of inferiority. For years he did not pick up a brush because he knew his work would never measure up to his competitors' work.

Perfectionism often worsens the quality of work. It is true that people are born with some qualities and abilities; however, people do not excel in their field only because of hard work. This is a myth that the society is slowly busting. Malcolm Gladwell said that it takes a person at least 10,000 hours to reach a certain level of greatness or genius in an industry. The artists that Joe had admired were in their late 50s, so they spent years making mediocre art before they made their masterpieces.

Inaction and Procrastination

When you want to be perfect at what you do, you may want to stop working on the task, and therefore procrastinate. When you compare yourself with others, and have high standards for yourself, you are not going to work better. You are shooting yourself in the foot.

Since you are afraid of failure, you stop trying. You forget that it takes at least a few failures before you become successful, and you choose to try nothing and accomplish nothing. You apply this fear to every aspect of your life. For instance, since you are socially awkward, you will refrain from meeting new people; however, only when you meet new people and make conversations can you overcome your shyness. If you avoid beating yourself up, you can develop some social skills soon. You should remember that it is okay to be bad at something, since that is the first step at being good at it.

Triggers of Guilt, Shame or Jealousy through Social Media

When you see how people are living their lives on Instagram and Facebook, you begin to feel inferior and start doubting yourself. For instance:

- You see that your friends at college are out partying and are socializing, while you stay at home.

- You see that all your friends are starting their families. This makes you question if you are making the right decisions.

- Your friends have many likes on their posts, but that makes you feel worthless or insignificant since you do not receive those many likes for your posts.

It is important to remember that people always use social media to present the perfect parts of their lives; therefore, you are always making a comparison of your life against one version of their life. You forget that these people have edited all the sad and boring parts of their life. Studies conducted on social media conclude that social media make people feel worse about themselves. This problem multiplies when you have an inferiority complex. A recent study concluded that using social media either during the day or night reduced the quality of sleep and led to increased anxiety, low self-esteem and depression.

Do not even get me started on magazines or news, since they only show images of the most attractive, wealthy and successful people.

You Judge Others

Let us look at some interesting patterns that you may have noticed. If you know men who have always been unsuccessful with women, they will begin to hate them. If a woman or man is thirty years old and still a virgin, she or he will be upset when they see a happy couple or a group of attractive men or women walk past them. This is because these groups of people remind them of what they feel inferior about – their looks, insecurities and fear of failure around the opposite sex.

When women look at newspapers or magazine covers, and find a skinny supermodel on the cover, she will worry about the unrealistic standards that the society has. She is not trying to understand what makes her mad. The image of the supermodel triggers the feelings of unworthiness and unattractiveness inside her. She may feel that she is not as valuable as the supermodel and not as attractive as she is; therefore, she believes that everybody judges her in the same way. Women believe that their value is solely dependent on their appearance.

Unlike women, men do not always compare their appearances, and nobody knows why. Numerous activists have started to petition against the images in magazines and newspapers. Have you observed the pattern yet? Let us look at one last example.

When people make fun of a millionaire wearing an expensive suit or driving an expensive car, they are trying to cover their feeling of inadequacy since they own a Toyota. However, if they win a lottery, they will certainly buy themselves an expensive car or suit; therefore, the lesson is that inferiority makes you judge another person. When you judge someone, you often try to make yourself feel better. This method backfires since you become spiteful. Start identifying the moments when you condemn other people and feel hateful. This will help you identify what makes you feel worse about yourself. Remember that what you perceive or feel about people around you is a reflection of the emotions and feelings within you. If you do not judge people often, you will not constantly feel judged.

Try to Hide Flaws without Success

People who are often insecure or feel ugly do not try to improve their appearance. They will certainly hide what they are ashamed of.

- They either wear baggy clothing to avoid looking at their body shape.

- Always strike the same pose in a photograph.

- If they have crooked teeth, they may try to avoid smiling at all. If they wear braces, they may either cover their mouth or stop smiling.

- If they feel ugly, women may wear a lot of makeup, but, then again, it differs from one woman to another.

The people in the examples above always worry about how people see them. They also want to control how society perceives them. You only feel stressed out and self-conscious from the constant need to stay alert.

Chapter Three: How to Stop Being Inferior

If you have an inferiority complex, you can use the strategies in this chapter that will help you get on the right track. You must be serious and ensure that you work on changing your life; therefore, you should start changing your behavior. Once you reach this chapter, you should implement the strategies mentioned in the book immediately.

Check Your Life Circle

The first thing you should do is to establish the parts of your life that are working, and those that are not. If you are doing great in your career, but do not have any confidence in your relationship, you should identify a way to improve that area of your life. Ensure that you learn to communicate better or listen better. It is always up to you to decide what part of your life you want to improve. When you change some parts of your life for the better, you will become a changed person.

Always Replace the Negativity

You may be uneducated, clumsy or overweight. That does not suggest that you are unintelligent, or that you cannot be kind to yourself. You must make a list of all the reasons why you put yourself down, and try to find a positive way to say it. Instead of calling yourself clumsy, you should tell yourself, "I have to learn to be more graceful."

You should also make sure that you identify the characteristics and traits that make you feel inferior. Identify the people around you that make you feel inferior. Is it your co-worker, a successful person, or your partner? How do these people make you feel bad about yourself? Is there a new skill you can develop that will help you feel better about yourself?

Your Complex can be Your Desire to be Like Someone Else

Stuart Killan

It is a great idea to look up to someone, or treat someone as your role model. You may want to learn from them, but you should avoid acting like them because you will lose your individuality. You cannot expect to impersonate someone and yet be who you are. Instead, you should identify the characteristics of the person you admire and try to emulate those characteristics while keeping your individuality. You should not compare yourself with them. Remember that you are you.

Stop Believing that a Flaw is the Root Cause to Your Problems

It is important to stop believing that every problem in your life is based on one of your flaws. This is an issue that many people face, and it is something they do not want to acknowledge. You must remember that your problems cannot be solved if you get married or lose weight. You must identify the root cause of the problem before you try to solve it.

Identify What Makes You Feel Good about Yourself

Do you feel inferior because you are short when compared to all your friends? You must know that this is not something you can do much about. Try to see what it is about you being short makes you feel inferior to others, and then analyze whether you can do something about this 'flaw.' Try to visualize what it would be like if you can be taller. Does that make you a happier person? Is it something you can relate to? Do you feel like yourself? Do you think you can become taller now?

You should use this technique to visualize your version of the solution. This will help you redefine your problem, and allow you to feel comfortable in your own skin. All you need to do is stay patient.

Ask Someone You Know to List Your Best Qualities

It is easier to ask someone you trust to list your favorite qualities. You know what they are, but you do not trust yourself. It feels great when someone lists your qualities. You will be more confident. There are times when you do not know who you are, but if a friend tells you what the best part about you is, you will feel better about yourself. If you want them to elaborate, ask them to do so. You may want to know why they think that you have a specific quality. Ask them to give you examples.

Focus on Your Successes

Regardless of what your age is, you should focus on your successes, small or big. Every great leader practices this regularly, and you should too. When you go to the gym, stay in touch with an old friend, complete all your tasks for the day or pack a healthy meal, congratulate yourself because they are worthy accomplishments. All of us have failures, but these failures are what help us become successful in the future. The truth is that you are doing better than you think.

People go through their day with the impression that every person around them knows what their flaws are. It is because of this that they feel inferior to the people around them; however, not everybody knows how clumsy you are, because they have their stuff to deal with. They may not have had the time in the world to consider your flaws. The truth is that most people around you are not thinking about you. If you think this is untrue, pay attention to the conversation you have when you are at a family gathering. Most people complain about how terrible their life is. They do not talk about your flaws; therefore, you are free.

Conclusion

Everybody feels inferior at some point in their life. There are many people who will do better than you, but you are doing much better than someone else. You should never let your inferiority complex get the better of you. Ensure that you push yourself to do better, and use that inferiority as a tool to drive you to do better. You must identify ways to develop confidence and use that confidence to be successful.

If you want to conquer your inferiority complex, you should focus on your self-talk, strengths and remember that nobody is watching you. The bottom line is that you can let go of your inferiority and be the best version of yourself without worrying too much about your life.

Thank you for purchasing this book. I hope you become confident and take over the world. I wish you good luck on your journey.

Confidence

The Nice Guy Myth - How to Get What You Want in Love and Life without Being a Pushover

By

Stuart Killan

Stuart Killan

Introduction

I want to thank you for purchasing the book, 'Shyness: The Nice Guy Myth - How to Get What You Want in Love and Life without Being a Pushover.'

People often believe that being nice is synonymous to being a pushover. It is because of this assumption that people who are nice are often advantage of. This may make you think twice about being nice to people. However, it does not have to be that way. You can be nice to people and still take a stand for yourself. If you want to learn how you can do this, you have come to the right place.

Over the course of the book, you will learn how you can be nice to people without being a pushover. You will learn about the things that you can do or say to avoid doing something that you do not want to.

I hope you gather all the information necessary.

Chapter One: What Makes You a Pushover

It is important to be nice if you want to be successful. This quality helps you maintain relationships since people will want to spend time with you; however, there is a thin line between being a pushover and being nice.

When you are too nice, you often make your way through life by placating the people around you. This makes it easy for people to push you over. You may want to take charge n many situations but are worried that you will come off as overbearing or having your opinion. This fear will make you submissive and give people the opportunity to extract work from you.

People who are pushovers often exhibit the characteristics listed below.

Pleasing

People often change their position or soften their opinion when they believe that the people around them will not receive their thoughts and opinions well. If you want to be successful, it is important that you communicate your thoughts and opinions. Instead of trying to please everybody, you should demand that they treat you with respect. If you try to please people in your workplace, you will realize that you are working on tasks that you do not want to do. You will find it difficult to tell people what you think about a specific task since they will not listen to what you have to say. Therefore, it is important that you educate yourself and become an expert in the field you are working in. This education will help you sound confident when you communicate your opinions.

Neediness

When you are too nice, you constantly seek approval from the people around you. It is important to remember that people cannot help you feel worthy. You cannot expect to succeed in life by coat-tailing another person. You can only succeed if you believe in yourself and are willing to stick to your beliefs regardless of what someone says to you. There are times when you need something from others. In those situations, ask yourself if you can get what you want without another's help. You must remember that what you want is important, and there are times when what you want will cause inconvenience to someone else. The only way you can get what you want is by saying what you want and going after it.

Exaggerating Compliments

It is hard to trust someone whose sentence begins and ends with a compliment. The same goes for you. Do not start and end a conversation with a compliment since that is manipulative. You only compliment these people since you are unable to handle your insecurities any other way. People often believe that they have secured another's approval if they feel good about it. You can only be successful when you are confident and not by pleasing another person.

Defensive

People will consider you weak when you are defensive. There are times when people will disagree with you. If you find it hard to deal with rejection, there is no path for you to succeed. You must develop resilience and accept criticism and feedback without being upset. People will not help you achieve success because they feel sorry for you. You must grow from constructive feedback.

Lying

When you have the innate need to please people, you become dishonest. You often agree with people when you do not believe in what they say. You should not be a parrot and accept or repeat everything they tell you. You will lose your identity. Your need to fit-in drives these actions. Successful people never try to fit in and are confident. They are strong to handle losses and are brutally honest whenever necessary.

Overworking

You overwork when you are desperate to prove your worth. When you have this attitude, you often work on tasks that you do not want to work on. When people sense that you are willing to do whatever it takes to prove your worth, they lose respect for you. You should learn to relax and do your part, and let others carry their weight.

You do not have to feel guilty about saying no, and you do not have to participate in activities that you do not want to do. Your answer will define your likes and dislikes and make you a distinct individual. People will know where you wish to stop and they will pick up the tasks from there. If people do not know these boundaries, they will often push you to do more.

Never Expressing Your Thoughts

People will not value you when you fail to express your opinions and thoughts. There will be times when people will not listen to you since they believe you do not have an opinion. Ensure that you never withhold your values and opinions.

You must realize that conflict is a part of success, and learn to state your opinions without worrying about what people may say. If you are worried that someone may reject your opinion, one can never know what your preferences are or who you truly are. Never look for agreement, and always state what you believe is true.

Uncertainty

People pleasers often ask for permission in situations where they do not need to ask for permission. They do this because they want to look respectful and polite; however, you look unintelligent since they believe that you cannot make the simplest decisions.

You must be bold and lead the way regardless of whether you are uncertain. People fall in line when you are bold. The best way to overcome uncertainty is to believe in commit to what you believe in and work towards that belief.

Apologetic

When you start every sentence with the word 'sorry,' it gives people the idea that you have low self-esteem. You should never apologize for your existence. When you begin the word with 'Sorry, but,' you give people the impression that you expect them to disapprove your opinion. Always start the sentence with "Listen," since that will ensure that people pay attention to what you are saying.

Never worry about making mistakes. It is better to make mistakes than to disappear. When you change your answers to please another person, you are not being true to yourself. Remember that nobody is perfect and you do not have to apologize. Your mistakes are your greatest teachers. So, learn from them.

Timid

When you are timid, you let the fear drive you away from your passion and happiness. Remember that you will never get anywhere by being timid and fearful. People are not sensitive and when you are timid. They will take advantage of you and will surpass you. You must find the confidence to pursue your passions. If you are timid, you follow your path aimlessly since you try to find a way to stay safe. Stay committed to your path.

The greatest irony is that when you are shy and timid, you allow people to do what they please with your life. To be successful, you must be confident about how you are or what you believe in. You must educate yourself and learn to be the best version of yourself. Keep learning until you reach the point where you have an opinion for yourself. You do not have to worry about whether you have the right opinion. Only when you embrace the differences, will you succeed. Remember that great ideas only come from debate. If you have some or all the qualities listed above, you should work towards changing how you think.

Chapter Two: How to Give Compliments

If you are shy, you will find it difficult to give compliments. People who are comfortable in situations always compliment the people around them. This chapter gives you some tips that will help you give good compliments and praise. It is important to learn this skill since it helps to start conversations and develop social bonds.

- Never give out compliments at random. If you do not believe in giving the compliment, you will come off as being insecure.

- Do not give a generic compliment. You should be specific about why you are giving them the compliment. For example, you can say, "Your eyes look beautiful" instead of saying "You look beautiful."

- Always consider the situation and the relationship you share with the person to ensure that the compliment is appropriate. If you want to give a comment that is personal, only give it to a friend in private.

- Always use creative words to compliment another. You can say, "Your dress looks beautiful and brings out the color of your eyes." Such compliments stick longer.

- Find opportunities to compliment a person's character and traits instead of the appearance since people do not listen to those compliments. For instance, you can compliment a teacher for his ability to motivate his students.

- Always give constructive criticism since a compliment always means more to the other person when he or she knows that you are being honest.

- Compliment people who are in authority. People at a higher position do not receive too many compliments and you will be surprised at the response you receive. Some people will willingly accept your compliment and welcome the feedback.

- When you compliment someone with low self-esteem, you should avoid inflated praise. Try to compliment their behavior and not their traits. Research shows that people with low self-esteem worry about their future when someone compliments their behavior.

When you have mastered the art of giving compliments, you will find that you are better at accepting them too. You must remember that you should always have a positive experience when you either give or receive compliments.

Chapter Three: How to Respond to Backhanded Compliments

Most backhanded compliments are mean-spirited; however, sometimes you may give backhanded compliments out of ignorance. People often give backhanded compliments when they are afraid that people will not accept them. They believe that it is cool to give backhanded compliments. When they give backhanded compliments, they do not have to worry about giving their true emotions away. Therefore, it is important to learn how to give backhanded compliments and how to respond to them.

Responding to Backhanded Compliments

Ignore it

Ignoring a comment does not necessarily mean that you allow someone to push you around. When you do not say anything, you do not give away your power. It only sends the message that you do not value the other person's opinion enough to defend yourself. You can also prevent an argument.

You should ignore people when you know they are saying something only to grab your attention. If someone says, "Thank you for the meal today. It is about time you cooked for me," do not react to it.

Thank them

You do not have to defend your choices to someone if they insult you, because your answer won't help the situation. Rather than arguing about why the compliment or comment hurt you, you can thank them and walk away. You should take this approach only when the other person is ignorant. For example, if your grandmother were to say, "It is better to work in a company than to work from home. I am glad that you no longer sit at home, but work in an actual office."

Only Acknowledge the Positive Portion

Criticism and feedback are essential to improve one's performance; however, it is counterproductive to sugar coat feedback with compliments. You must acknowledge only the positive portion of the compliment to show the person that you do not accept passive-aggressive comments. For example, your boss may say, "It was wonderful to see how well you worked today. It would have been great had you worked the same last week." All you need to do is thank the person for observing how well you worked today.

Address the Insult

Backhanded compliments have a negative effect on relationships. Therefore, it is best to acknowledge the issue directly. Otherwise, the comments can become snarky, which will affect your relationship. If you do not want hurtful comments to come in the way of your relationship, you should speak up. If your friend says, "This dress looks wonderful on you. It hides your curves." Respond to your friend by telling him or her what part of that comment hurt you. If the compliment comes as a surprise to you, address it later.

Always Keep Your Sense of Humor

There are times when you should not take the comments some people make too seriously. These people may either not know how to deal with their emotions or want to hurt you. You can respond with a little humor. Do not be snobbish. For example, if a colleague says, "Congratulations on the work trip to Switzerland. Maybe now you will be happy about work." You can respond to that colleague by saying, "Haha, thank you, but it sounds like you are happy to see me leave."

Chapter Four: Why should You Avoid Exaggerated Compliments

People welcome compliments if they do not sound insincere. It feels great if someone recognizes you for the work that you do or who you are. Most people succeed when they receive compliments since they can warm their hearts, drive away fear and self-doubt and give us confidence; however, praise has negative effects too. Often, praise is verbal bribery, and a person offers it only when he or she knows it will work in his favor. In this chapter, you will learn why you must avoid giving exaggerated compliments.

If you are insecure and require confirmation from external sources to feel good, you are susceptible to insincere praise that has a price attached to it. People often prey on those with low self-esteem, and they are adept at detecting such people. They know what to say to build your confidence and use you for their own benefit. This does not mean that you should be suspicious of the people around you. But, there are times when it would be a good idea to consider whether someone is praising you for their benefit. If someone's compliments are exaggerated or overblown, they have an ulterior motive, and you should find a way to understand their true intentions.

Let us look at six reasons why flattery and praise may sometimes be schemes to use you.

- If people are insecure, they will compliment you in a way that helps them fit better into your social cycle. There are some people who agree to everything you say to win your favor. If you are someone who does this, you must stop immediately. As mentioned earlier, you should never agree with something anybody says to secure your relationship with them. You should stay true to your opinion.

- Some people butter you up before they bring you to the bargaining table. They do this to ensure that you will agree to their bargain. These people ensure that they praise you enough to make you feel special, regardless of how you see yourself. Eventually, you will be willing to compromise with them and will bend yourself to their will. This is because you believe you are in a mutually beneficial relationship.

- There are times when people may praise you to extract a specific favor from you. This is closely related to the point mentioned above. They praise you to increase the possibility that you will comply with their needs. They will gift you with praise and flattery, which will compel you to agree to their needs and desires. It is easy for them to take advantage of you to fulfill some deep desire. You may also lap up this praise since it fulfills your need to fit in. In such situations, you will find it difficult to differentiate between genuine and fake compliments.

- If you have fallen out with the person because of his or her behavior, they may resort to flatter to get back in your good books. If they can make you feel vindicated or supported, you will feel better about them. The probability that you will forgive them will increase when you fall for their insincere praises. You may then give the relationship a second chance or maybe a third.

- If people are unethical or shameless, they will offer you praise to ensure that you confide in them alone. You may also feel 'comfortable' about sharing some important information with them. Once they have this information, they will use it against you, either passively or aggressively depending on the situation. They will take advantage of the position they are in by betraying your trust and pursuing their agenda. In the workplace, this can mean that the person will steal the promotion that you should receive. When you trust their praise, they have the chance to trick you into their confidence and exploit your trust in them.

- Another reason people compliment others is to manipulate them into behaving in a specific way. For example, in the Big Bang Theory, Sheldon gives Penny a treat every time she behaves 'well'. Most people give exaggerated compliments because they want you to comply with their whims and fancies. These praises will make you believe that you are good or worthy only when you behave the way people expect you to. This type of behavior leads to psychological abuse.

Chapter Five: Why Should You Laugh at Yourself

Research has shown that it is healthy to laugh at yourself. A study conducted by a team at the Mind, Brain and Behavior Research Center in Spain concluded that a person is happier when he or she makes self-deprecating jokes. This conclusion contradicts many other studies previously conducted on this topic since self-deprecating jokes were closely associated with poor mental health.

Jorge Torres Marin said that one could only make jokes about themselves if he or she is happy and social to an extent. The specifics of the findings are dependent on where you live. If people around you are comfortable with laughing at themselves, you may find it easier to laugh at yourself. Therefore, Marin wants to conduct more research on the topic to create a map of where one can feel free to laugh at themselves. He believes that culture plays an important role in this instance.

Marin mentioned that the phrase 'sense of humor' led to negative conclusions in previous studies. Many cultures define the phrase differently, which made it difficult for early research to understand why self-deprecating humor is good for you. There are two reasons why it was difficult to conclude this.

- Not everybody finds the same topics funny. If people are of different cultures, they will certainly find different subjects funny. For example, someone from England may not find baseball humor funny, but someone from the USA will find those jokes funny if he or she does not support the team.

- Another reason it was difficult to study humor was that people express it differently. Different behavior and a variety of comments can be humorous, and this variety overwhelmed researchers. This made it difficult to conclude why it is good for one to laugh at himself or herself.

However, Marin and his team did not create any boundaries while working on their hypothesis. Another researcher from the team, Hugo Dios, said that their research aimed to overcome every boundary. Marin and his team-studied behavior related to humor and classified that humor into adaptive and harmful humor. They broke different styles and types of humor down and explained that adaptive humor helped to strengthen relationships; however, self-enhancing humor only worked in stressful situations.

These styles of humor are closely related to a person's physiological wellbeing and can also be related to concepts like depression and anxiety. The team concluded that people who laugh at themselves know how to curb anger, but they cannot manage anger well. Therefore, it is acceptable to laugh at yourself occasionally. It shows people that you do not mind making fun of yourself.

Chapter Six: How to Make Fun of Others without Hurting Them

It is a good way to make friends by learning to tease people the right way; however, you should make sure that the other person shares the same sense of humor as you. You can also make fun of others if they are mean to you or to the people around you. Conversations flow with hilarity when you tease your friends.

Teasing Your Friends

When you tease your friends, you can be sarcastic. When you use sarcasm, you imply that your friend is being silly by asking you a reasonable question.

- You can twist your answer when someone asks you a question.

- Give your friends answers that are obviously wrong.

- Try to exaggerate any response.

Differentiate between Fun and Cruelty

It is funnier and better to tease someone about something that is not the truth. If you have a friend who gets bad grades do not call him or her out in front of everybody else. He or she may be sensitive about it and it is cruel to draw attention to it. However, if your friend is a straight A's student, you can make fun of how bad he studies because that is the exact opposite of who he is.

Make Fun of their Intelligence

You can tease someone about how smart they are. If you know that the person does not mind if you make fun of their intelligence, go ahead and crack appropriate jokes. For example, you can say, "Please stop talking now. We are becoming wiser."

Use Metaphors and Similes

You can use some weird metaphors and similes to make fun of someone. These do not have to make sense, but people will laugh their heart out if the similes are weird. If someone is constantly annoying you, you can say, "You are like the Hulk of being extremely annoying."

React Dramatically

There are times when you do not have to say anything to make fun of your friend. You can react dramatically to something your friend said as if it is the silliest thing you have ever heard. Exhale loudly, let your head fall backward, pretend you are asleep or roll your eyes.

Know When to Joke

It is important to learn when to crack a joke or make fun of someone. The timing can help someone differentiate between whether a person takes a joke in good faith. You must wait for the right opportunity to make a sarcastic comment. Pause after the joke to see how your friend received it. If he or she is upset, apologize to them immediately.

Know When to Stop

It is important to know when to stop. You cannot make fun of people or take it too far. Ensure that the person you are making fun of knows that you are joking. If you notice that they have taken the joke personally, stop. You should never hurt someone by picking on them. If someone is upset, apologize to them right away and let them know that you were only making fun of

Stuart Killan

them.

Learn to Take it Well

If you make fun of people, they will make fun of you too. Learn to take it in the right stride. If you react negatively to every joke made about you, people will not speak to you or make fun of you.

Conclusion

Thank you once again for purchasing the book.

People believe that a person who is shy is a pushover and they take advantage of it. These people use that quality until it benefits them. If you are shy, you may have noticed that people make you do work that you do not want to do and do not listen to your opinions. It is time you change that.

Over the course of this book, you will learn how you can be a nice person without being a pushover. If you use the techniques mentioned in this book, you will never come across as a mean person.

I hope you have gathered all the information you are looking for.

Conversation

The Small Talk Solution – How to Handle Small Talk as an Introvert and Never Run Out of Things to Say

By

Stuart Killan

Introduction

I want to thank you for choosing this book, 'Shyness: The Small Talk Solution - How to Handle Small Talk as an Introvert and Never Run Out of Things to Say' and I hope you find it informative and interesting.'

Shyness is a quality that is common among 40% of adults around the world. Being shy can make it difficult for people to make social connections, and lead to a social anxiety disorder.

One way of beating shyness is by engaging in small talk. Small talk refers to making small conversations with random people in order to get to know them better, as well as increasing your social circle; however, it is not easy to engage in small talk. I'm sure you have had experiences where you had to force every single word you said to someone. This happens because it takes a little time and effort to become good at small talk, and going into it without preparation can often lead to forced conversations.

There is a plethora of small talk topics to choose from, and can prove to be a good conversation starter between two people. If you happen to have a social anxiety disorder, then engaging in small talk can be especially nerve-racking. In such a case, you have to make the effort of being a little more confident in your approach, and touching on topics that are relevant.

Small talk mostly involves being prepared and knowing exactly what to say. You must make it a point to overcome your fears and talk to people confidently. This book will act as your guide to small talk, and teach you some of the ways in which you can, effortlessly, engage in it.

Let us begin!

Chapter One: Three Reasons Why Small Talk Matters

In this first chapter, we will look at the three main reasons for engaging in small talk.

Learn About Someone New

It is obvious that all human beings are curious and love to know what other people do, think, and like etc. Engaging in small talk can help you learn about others and their likes and dislikes. Would it not feel nice to know about someone and what they are all about? You will have a new person to connect with, and discuss topics that are common between the two of you.

See if there's a Relationship there You Want to Pursue - Friendship/Professional/Dating etc.

Human beings thrive on relationships. Humans are fine-tuned to find other like-minded humans, be it friends, partner, or lover etc. When you engage in small talk, you never know the kind of relationship you can establish with the other person, be it friendship, professional connect or simply date them.

Have a Fun, Enjoyable Conversation

Engaging in small talk can make you happy. You will feel much better about yourself and have an enjoyable time talking to others. Conversations will give you something to think about. You will have more things to ponder over and discuss.

It is key to engage in small talk so that you are able to widen your mental horizons. You will benefit from it by making more relevant connections and talk to more interesting people on a daily basis.

Through the course of this book, you will read about some of the best topics to talk on, and how asking relevant questions can keep you engaged without getting bored for a long time.

Chapter Two: Complimenting in Small Talk

Giving and receiving compliments can feel great. It tells someone that you like them and appreciate them.

As per studies, those who approach others with a compliment are more likely to succeed at small talk, so it is best to learn how to compliment someone. Here are two aspects of complimenting someone:

Appearance

One of the best ways to compliment someone is by telling them how nice they look. It can be about their hair, make-up, dressing style, or their handbag etc.

Performance

These compliments are about telling people that they have done a good job at something.

Keep it Genuine

It is obvious that all of us feel good when compliments come our way. We have all received at least one compliment in our lives, and it has only made us feel great about ourselves but, a compliment can only be appreciated when it comes from the heart and is genuine. That is, the compliment does not have any strings attached. You must not compliment someone just to get a conversation going as, in most cases, people will be able to tell whether it was genuine or not.

People love to pay others a compliment. In fact, it is a part of the culture in many European countries. Both giving and taking a compliment is very important, especially if you plan on establishing a lasting relationship with someone.

If you are not genuine, then the receiver might not be able to connect with you. Say, for example, you spot a friend wearing a dress that is unflattering. Just because it is a new dress does not mean you tell them it is looking great, as that can sound fake. You can choose to remain silent.

The point is to make the receiver feel good about something. This will especially feel good to both when the receiver is least expecting a compliment. It is a great idea to compliment one person in your life every day. It will make them feel great. You need not always compliment them without something elaborate. Even a simple "Hi, I love your shoes" will make them feel good or appreciated. It will cost you nothing and, as they say, you get what you give.

Complimenting Someone

Before you compliment someone, try to observe them for some time. Doing so can help you know what they like and what will work best on them. For example, if you observe someone and they keep pushing their hair back or keep adjusting it, then it means that they would like to be complimented for their great hair. Doing so can not only help you get started with a conversation, but also talk about topics such as what shampoo they use, and where they get their coloring done etc.

Grabbing Attention

An important aspect associated with small talk is grabbing someone's attention. You have to approach them in such a way that they take notice of you going towards them. Once you reach them, put forth the compliment in an assertive manner, such that they realize they have been observed and you are paying them a compliment based on your best asset. It will show that you have made an effort from your end.

Make sure the compliment is genuine. They have to understand that you are not just friendly, but also very genuine towards others.

Cynics

Be open to the idea that not everybody you compliment will take it in the right spirit. There will always be cynics. You must not blame them or go about back biting them just because they did not accept your compliment. That would make you look quite bad, so it is best to leave a situation as it is when someone is not receptive to your compliment. At the same time, if someone pays you a compliment, and you learn they have been backbiting you, you must accept it and forget it instead of harping over it, as it will take away from the compliment you received and how you felt upon receiving it. Sometimes, it is best to focus just on the positives of things so that you can be more open to accepting compliments and receptive of them.

Rejecting Compliments

If you are new to a place, it is obvious that you will have to adopt an entirely new culture. Not everyone will be receptive of your compliments, especially if they are not sure what you meant, or they are uncomfortable receiving a compliment out of the blue from a stranger or a foreigner. In such a case, you must not be disheartened if they just leave you with a weird stare as if to say they disapprove of your compliment. It does not mean that they did not like the compliment; it just means that they are taking some time accepting it and that they will be more receptive to it as time passes. You must definitely keep paying them compliments and do it often so that it becomes easier to pass compliments to people.

On the flipside, you might not be interested in receiving a compliment from everyone who comes your way. It can be a little uncomfortable to receive it from someone who you cannot compliment back. You have to make sure that you are cordial with them, and just a friendly nod can make it seem genuine and that you appreciate what they are saying to you. Remember that small talk is a two-way street. The more receptive you are to others approaching you, the more you will feel confident to do the same. You have to develop enough self-confidence to be able to accept what others say to you.

To put it simple, small talk will be more meaningful and easier to engage in when there are compliments involved. It sets a standard and you will feel like talking more with someone who is on the same page as you. Remember that you will be setting an example for someone; it can be your children, sibling, or friends etc, so the kind of effort you put in and the pay-off you receive, will all reflect on how you set the standard for them to follow.

Stuart Killan

You must make use of the right body language skills to make sure that it is easier for people to be comfortable in your presence and talk more freely with you.

Chapter Three: High-Quality Questions: Ask Them Something That Gets Them Talking Forever

When it comes to making small talk, you have to be in a position to ask all the right questions that can get the conversations going. Ensure that you have a list of questions ready that you can bring up throughout the length of the conversation so that the listener is engaged.

To help you out, here is a list of questions you can ask someone so that the conversation is always interesting. There is widespread misconception that small talk has to be limited to shorter questions that solicit one-word answers, but this is not true at all. It is best to ask questions that are meaningful and make the other person answer in an elaborate manner.

What Generally Excites You?

This is a great question to get a conversation going. The best part about this question is that it can be about people's work life, about their personal life, or social life etc. There can be many ways in which this question can be answered. Once they answer it based on one aspect of their life, you have to quickly ask them about another aspect and so on to make it interesting.

What do You Look Forward to?

Once they tell you what excites them in life, you can ask them what they look forward to having next. This too can be an interesting question with many answers.

What is the Best thing that's Come Your Way Recently?

This question can make the conversation quite interesting. It will get the listener to ponder over his or her recent life and what has come their way. It opens up the thought process and tells them that you are open to receiving information from them. It also lets you find common interests.

What's the Most Important Thing You Want to Tell Me about You?

This might sound like a personal question, but asking it can make you open up better to the other person and vice versa. It is best to avoid this question as the first thing to ask someone. Give them time to adjust or ease into the conversation before asking them this direct question.

What is Your Story?

It is obvious that you will want to know their story and them know yours, so get the ball rolling by asking them what their story is. Some fun stories deal with knowing funny incidents about them; their foreign travels, or talking about their tattoos etc. This question can open up many possibilities and hours of discussions.

Describe a Defining Moment of Your Life?

This is an important question to ask someone you are engaging in small talk with. It builds a momentum and the listener goes a little deep into thought. It can be a very comfortable way of going into someone's personal life without being too pushy or trying to dig deep.

What was it about Your Profession that Attracted You?

When it comes to having small talk, it is important not to bombard someone with questions that are too much to think about from the get-go. If you ask someone what they do as the very first question, they might feel a little apprehensive to answer it right away or give you an incomplete answer. In such a case, you have to drop the question only after you have reached a level of comfort with them. Many people will not be happy about their job, and you can offer them advice or counsel them.

What Books have You been Reading Lately?

Talking about books and authors is always a great way to break the ice or keep a conversation going. Even if you do not actively read, there will always be one or two authors common between you, especially if the listener is a reader. You can ask them for recommendations and recommend books to them. You can talk on genres that are common, and how they interpreted a certain book.

How can I be of Help to You Right Now?

In order to make it interesting and to show that you really care for them, ask them how you can make it better for them or of what help you can be to them. It can be both personally or professionally. You will notice that this has made them quite happy and that they are more responsive to you after you have made this suggestion. You will see that you will be able to find people who are genuine and are genuinely interested in keeping in touch with you.

You have to be sincere and showcase a genuine interest in being of help to the person. Don't say it if you will not be able to help them.

These are just some of the fun questions that you can ask, but you are not limited to just these. Ask them other questions that are open-ended and you will see how smooth sailing your conversation goes.

Chapter Four: Being Prepared, Keeping It Fun

Before engaging in small talk, you have to ensure that you are prepared for it. Going into a conversation without proper preparation can make it a little boring or too forced. Here are some pointers to help you keep the conversations more relevant and interesting:

Be Prepared

Do not approach a person if there is nothing much to talk about or are unprepared with topics to discuss. Approach them only after you have come up with at least 3 or 4 questions to discuss. You have to be prepared to ask questions that will solicit a reply and keep the conversation going. We looked at some of the questions to ask in the previous chapter. Apart from them, you can also consider asking, for example, "What brings you to this part of town?" "What are your plans for summer?" The idea is to learn more about the person to get a conversation going, and have enough back-up questions to ask after you are done with the first set of questions.

Comfort

Pay attention to comfort at all times. Remember that you have to make someone feel comfortable and feel at ease when you approach them. You have to think for another person and how they will feel when approached by a stranger. Maintain a friendly approach and show them that you are keenly listening to everything they have to say to you. Keep nodding and use expressions such as "hmmmm" to show that you are paying attention to whatever they are saying. Reply to them often so that they know you have their attention. Do not think too much when the other person is talking. Allow them to finish talking before thinking of your response. Take your time thinking about the response, and don't simply say something just for the sake of it.

Although asking and receiving questions is always a good idea, you have to ensure that you do not ask certain questions that can be too personal. Some of them include asking about their family, their health issues, or political views etc. Everyone can be quite opinionated about these, and asking about them can make them uncomfortable. It might also lead to unnecessary fights and arguments so keep politics and religion out of your conversations, and stick to something that is more relevant to the situation and is common between you.

Do not think that it is not ok to oppose some of their thoughts. If you have an opinion that goes against their thoughts, then you can put it forth. You should listen to what they have to say and then tell them what you think. Remember that it is not your job to convince them about something, and all you can do is be honest with them.

If you are planning to have a small talk with someone from the office, then the topics have to be pretty neutral. If the topics are controversial, you may not be able to approach the person freely in the future to have a discussion. You may not even gain anything worthwhile from the conversation.

If in case things do get uncomfortable, consider changing the subject to something that can fill in the gaps between the conversations. Allow them to counter your argument before saying "That's an interesting point of view" before changing the topic.

If in case your listener happens to bring up a topic that is not agreeable to you, be polite and tell them that it is best not to further discuss it. Let them finish saying what they have to say, and tell them that your opinions might clash and it is best to talk about something more relevant to you. Stick with neutral topics for at least the first two to three conversations.

If you wish to break away from them just so that you do not have to indulge further in conversation with them, tell them "It was nice talking to you, and I will get back to you after I am done with my work." It will not seem rude, and you will give them time to think about other topics to talk about. Make sure you go straight back to work and not strike up a conversation with someone else as that might come across as rude.

Don't Make it about Yourself

It is important not to make things about yourself. You will end up killing the conversation in no time. Nobody wants to hear about you all the time. You have to limit the conversation to a sentence or two about you and no more. There is no point in going about just your side of the story as you might bore yourself after some time.

If the conversation is starting to get a little redundant, consider telling them a story or an anecdote about you to lighten the mood and take you out from an awkward territory.

If you feel that they are talking too much about themselves, stop them after about 5 minutes of them starting. Interrupt them by introducing a new topic that has relevance to the current one. Ask them questions that do not relate to their personal life. Talk about something that is a part of the room. Bring up topics that are more in keeping with whatever is currently trending, or a part of the current setting.

Join a Group

A great way to connect with like-minded people is by joining a group where there are people who talk on topics that are of relevance to you. Toastmasters can prove to be a great place for you to start talking and meeting new people. Find one in your area and regularly partake in the discussions and events. There can be other platforms too where you can connect with people and engage in small talk. You should capitalize on any opportunity that comes your way. It will only make you go about having small talk in a smoother manner.

Chapter 5: Getting their Opinion/Advice on Something

Small talk need not always be limited to talking about general things. You can always ask them for something or seek advice on something.

Asking for Advice

If you want to get started with small talk with someone, it is a good idea to seek advice. You can ask them about their personal life experiences or what they have faced in their life. Try to relate to it and see how it has been for you personally. Seek their advice on a topic that has been bugging you. Even if they are unable to give you appropriate advice, you at least have someone to talk to about some of your concerns.

Make sure the topics aren't too personal, like asking them whether you should separate from your partner. Such topics should not be discussed with people you wish to have small talk with. Reserve it for someone who is a little closer to you.

Also, avoid seeking advice on topics that happen to be your favorites. If they advise you to go against your liking, you might feel offended and not respect their opinions.

Approach them with a casual nature and start with something like, "Hey, I have a quick question for you." This sets the right tone for the conversation.

Once you have asked them the question, allow them time to think about it and then answer. If they impulsively tell you something, it means they haven't given it a thought and might not be able to give you the best advice.

Consider paraphrasing it for them so that they understand what it is that you seek from them. Elaborate it if need be.

Once they give you their advice, do not be in a hurry to implement it. Counter it with an argument to check whether the advice is good or not.

On the other hand, if someone is seeking advice from you, listen to what they have to ask and think about it for some time. Do not be impulsive with your response. If you think you are not the right person to answer it, or are not qualified enough, tell them the same in a polite manner.

Conclusion

I thank you once again for choosing this book and hope you had a good time reading it.

The main aim of this book was to teach you how small talk can help you become a better person. You can put an end to your social awkwardness and anxiety just by engaging in small talk.

All it takes is a little effort from your end. Once you get the hang of it, you will start to have conversations more freely. You will begin to speak more meaningfully and be in a better position to accept compliments and criticism.

I urge you to go through the book once more so that you understand what it takes to have small talk with others. I hope you have a great time engaging in small talk and talking to others.

Public Speaking

How to Improve Your Speaking Voice in Just 15 Minutes

By

Stuart Killan

Introduction

I want to thank you for choosing this book, '*Shyness: How To Improve Your Speaking Voice In Just 15 Minutes*' and hope you find the book informative and interesting.

Shyness is a common human tendency. According to a survey, about 40% of adults experience shyness on a day-to-day basis. It is safe to say that almost everyone will, at one point in their life, experience shyness. Shyness extends over a wide spectrum of possibilities, including socially withdrawn, socially anxious, and socially isolated etc.

If you happen to be just a little shy, then you will remain a little uncomfortable in a social setting. You will also find it tough to start a conversation with someone. If you happen to be a lot shyer, you will prefer to be socially isolated and despise the thought of making conversation with people.

An important aspect of being able to open up socially is having a strong voice. A strong voice can give you the confidence to approach people in a better way.

If you happen to be a shy person with a weak voice and it is causing you anxiety or making you too self-conscious, then you have come to the right place. This book will serve as your guide to teach you the importance of enhancing your speaking voice so that you can talk more freely with people around you.

The book takes you through a few voice enhancement-based exercises that you can practice in order to improve your speaking voice and help you stave off your social anxiety limitations.

Let us begin!

Chapter One: Breathing Exercises

When it comes to enhancing your speaking voice, you have to carry out a few breathing exercises in order to make it easier for you to speak efficiently. These exercises are directed towards your abdominal muscles in order to improve your voice. The key is to pay attention to the breathing, and listening to the air moving in and out of your lungs. You can carry out these exercises once a day for at least two weeks to see any improvement in your voice.

Here are some of the exercises to carry out:

Exercise one

- Lie down on your back and place a book over your stomach or just your hands.

- Draw in a deep breath through your mouth and feel the book or your hands rising up.

- Release the breath through your mouth and feel the book moving down.

- You have to be able to breathe in and out without much effort.

Exercise two

- Sit on a chair and place your feet firmly on the ground.

- Push your shoulders backwards and sit straight.

- Place a hand over your stomach and breathe in from your nose and out from your mouth.

- You have to feel your stomach moving in and out.

- Your upper body must remain steady and you can consider sitting in front of a mirror while taking up this exercise.

- Draw the breath in from your nose and release it from your mouth.

- While doing so, begin humming by reciting "hummm."

- The vibrations should move all throughout your body and especially around your nose area.

- The sound should originate from your nose and not your lungs.

- Now, release the air through your mouth and utter "up" or "hup."

Exercise three

- Sit on a chair with your shoulders pulled back.

- Draw in breaths from your mouth while saying "up one, up two, up three" until "up ten."

- You have to draw in a breath after each phrase.

- Once you start getting comfortable with it, you have to repeat the words faster.

- An alternative to this method is to sit with a straight back and your shoulders pushed back.

- Breathe in and out through your nose and say "run a mile" "get a paper" or "buy some food."

- Release the breath from your mouth.

Exercise four

- Sit on the chair with your shoulders pushed backwards.

- Breathe in and out from your mouth while reading a book out loud.

- Hold your breath for 10 syllables and then breathe out and so on.

Apart from these, there are some basic exercises that can help you warm up your voice. They are as follows:

- Stand straight and exhale all the air from your lungs and keep pushing it out until you feel like everything is out.

- Once all the air has been pushed out, you will automatically start to inhale and draw in deeper breaths.

- You have to visualize how the air enters your lungs, and imagine it as being food for your hungry lungs.

- Keep repeating this for about three to four times.

- Next, exhale the air out comfortably.

- Follow it by taking in a deep breath but not pushing your limit.

- Hold it in for about 15 seconds before releasing it.

- Increase the holding time to 30 seconds, followed by 45 seconds and so on.

- Continue to do so until you can hold your breath for an entire minute.

- This exercise is carried out in order to strengthen your diaphragm and the muscles around it.

- Next up, stand erect and draw in five deep breaths with an open mouth.

- You will see that you are unable to do so without using your diaphragm.

- Once your lungs are full, release the air through your nose and your mouth closed.

- Next, let out a hearty laugh and "ha ha" as loudly as you can.

- Laugh out your inhaled breath and, once everything is exhaled, quickly draw in a deep breath.

- Next up, close your lips tightly and laugh through your nose without making a sound.

- Your diaphragm will expand and contract accordingly.

- Next up, stand straight and bend down to touch your toes.

- Do not try to exert too much pressure while doing so and go down gently.

- Remain still for 1 to 2 minutes.

- Breathe out and go back to the erect position.

- Stand straight and place your hands over your hips and push your shoulders backwards and try to look at the ceiling and yawn.

- Your waist should expand and your diaphragm should inflate and deflate to let the air in and out.

- Exhale the breath out to produce an "om" sound.

- Next up, stand straight and draw in deep breaths and, as you release the breath, count from one to five in a single breath.

- Once you are comfortable, count from one to ten in a single breath, but make sure you do not strain your vocal chords and the air moves in and out effortlessly.

- Open a book and read a combination of long and short sentences within a single breath.

Remember not to fill up your lungs too much before speaking as it can make you feel uncomfortable. Your mind will always tell you when you should stop and you should listen to it. Your breath should be easy to control and keep you comfortable. Yawning can help you release some of the tension in your neck and jaw and thus, yawn before you speak to someone just to be free.

When it comes to carrying out some of these in public, you have to be subtle about it so that people do not notice it. If you are giving a speech, then you must control your breath in such a way that the microphone does not pick up on it.

Chapter Two: Resonation

Resonation plays an important role in giving you the confidence to speak freely and approach someone more authoritatively.

What is Resonance?

Resonance refers to the amplification of sound. It is meant to adjust the timbre of your voice by stressing on specific vocal qualities over others. To put it simply, resonators help to make tone quality better by brightening and warming them up. It increases the volume and the start sound. It is like a recital hall where people sitting in all corners can clearly hear the voice of the singer singing on the stage.

It is important to create a well resonating voice so that everybody can hear it and you have good control over it.

Where does Vocal Resonance Occur?

Resonance occurs in the pharyngeal cavity and is a part of the nasal cavities, throat, mouth and larynx. The names for these areas are known as laryngopharynx, oropharynx, and nasopharynx.

Although there are other cavity resonators in the body that help to create vocal sounds, they are usually not considered to be easy to control. For example, the trachea can produce a grunting sound, but cannot be controlled. Lungs and bronchi make vibrations and so do the laryngeal cavities. These reflect the sound, vibrate and resonate like sounding boards. Essentially speaking, everything that lies in between the head and the chest tend to enhance vocal resonance. Even singers do not have a control over the resonators but can feel the vibrations.

What is Laryngopharynx Resonance?

The laryngopharynx is a part of the throat and lies between the top of the larynx and the bottom of the tongue and adds warmth to the voice. This area has muscles and tubes around it. Singers have the capability of switching up the diameter and the length of the laryngopharynx, but not its shape. Having a higher larynx can shorten the tube and a lower larynx can lengthen it. One that lies in between is best for singers with the tube remaining four to five inches long. The diameter is usually large and disengages the muscles inside the tube.

Adding Warmth and Volume

If you happen to be someone whose voice is quite bright and would like to improve your tone, then you have to focus on laryngopharynx resonance, but do not over-stress it as it can lead to a sunken tone. The key is to enlarge the diameter of your throat by lowering the larynx and relaxing your throat. To do this, close your mouth and draw in a deep breath like you are about to yawn. You have to feel the larynx expand. You must adopt a neutral laryngeal pose that is not any higher than, or is slightly lower than, your usual speaking voice.

You have to stress on the "ah" while feeling the breath go deep just like you feel before yawning. If your resonance increases, then your volume and warmth will increase too.

What is Oropharynx Resonance?

The oropharynx happens to be the gap from the bottom of the tongue towards the soft palate. The mouth and the jawline, along with the lips, tend to determine this area's shape and size. When you lower the jaw, you tend to increase the gap, and when you close the jaw, you tend to decrease the gap. If you press the back of the tongue against the back of the mouth, then it produces a humming sound as it prevents air from going through the mouth. It is this very area where consonants are generated. Adjusting this area is what helps you speak but, if only this area is used while making a speech, it can be inconsistent and wonky.

Adding Brightness and Volume to Your Voice Using Nasopharynx Resonance

When it comes to adding brightness to your voice, it is important not to close off the space in the nasopharynx, especially while singing upscale. The best way to determine nasopharynx resonance is by pinching your nostrils while singing.

You will notice that some consonants are difficult and nearly impossible to sing, as they need larger amounts of air to move through the nostrils. These happen to be consonants such as "m" "n" and "ng." In case your voice happens to stress on these three consonants in particular, it means that you speak nasally. Instead, if there seem to be vibrations occurring in the bridge of your nose when you touch it, then you speak with a nasopharynx resonance.

Chapter Three: Don't Forget Silence

Silence happens to be a very powerful tool that can be used when speaking to someone. Pausing can help you lay emphasis on your charismatic nature and not make you look like someone who cannot stop babbling. It gives people the time to understand what you are saying and absorb your ideas.

Here is how you can use speech to your advantage:

Pausing between Major Parts of Speech

Remember that your audience will only be able to process your speech when it comes in smaller or more manageable pieces. A disadvantage associated with public speaking is that people tend to present one major point after another without stopping, thereby overloading the audience. This means that the listener is receiving too much data without a proper break and a conclusion. The speech should be such that there should be a structure to it and a pause or silence in between each to divide it.

Silence Helps Your Audience Absorb More Information

When it comes to telling your listener something important that you want him or her to absorb and retain, you must use the power of silence to do so. If you happen to pause at the right time to help the listener process the information, the audience will respond to it in real time. Remember that they are not reading a book where they can simply re-read a paragraph to grasp it. A short stint of silence can help them grasp the main point and analyze it in their mind.

Use of Dramatic Pause

A dramatic pause is a tool used by stage actors during performances. This pause is taken at a time when the audience is expecting something important and binds together the entire conversation and, just when the crucial line or piece of information is delivered, the audience bursts into a thunderous clap. Similarly, you have to take a pause just when your listener gets very excited to hear what you have to say, which can impact the whole speech. Remember that the length of the pause will always seem longer to you than your listener so you have to drag it just enough for the listener to feel like the gap was just right.

Ask a Question and then Go Quiet

When you wish to engage the listener, you have to ask them many questions. In fact, you have to ask them relevant questions that you want answers to. Apart from them, you must also ask questions to which they will not have an answer to and go quiet. This will make them think and will grab their attention. You have to pause until such time as they come up with an answer.

Using Silence to Control the Pace

When you speak to someone, it is important to make sure that you go about it at the right speed. If you are too fast, the listener will not understand you and, if you are too slow, the listener will get bored so it is important to make use of pauses to ensure that you control the pace at which you speak. If you pause for no reason, the listener will think you are nervous so it is best to know when to take a pause to make the speech more impactful.

Chapter Four: Articulation

The power of articulation is often undermined when developing a strong speech. In order to understand articulation, you have to pay attention to the following variables:

Pitch Variation

You must vary the pitch and work on the high and low frequencies of your voice in order to engage the listener and keep them interested in what you say.

Voice Projection

When it comes to voice projection, you have to be able to speak with certain intensity, such that people who are even 20 feet away can clearly hear you. This intensity should be such that people know exactly what you are saying so that all their attention is moved towards you.

Using Pauses

As discussed in the previous chapter, using pauses is crucial to make a big impact. You must place strategic pauses in your speech to ensure that the listener understands the intensity of the speech.

Sentence Length Variation

An important aspect associated with delivering a powerful speech is about mixing up the length of the sentence. You must alternate between long and short sentences to make it easier for the listener to understand what you are saying. If you bombard them with long sentences, it will confuse them so make sure it is a mixture of the two.

Sound of Your Voice

The sound of your voice can make a big difference when it comes to making an impact on your listener. In order to know how your voice sounds to someone, record something and listen to it. Analyze how it makes you feel. Note the positives and the negatives. Understand whether it makes someone feel happy or annoyed. Determine whether you have to work on the tone etc.

Speed Variation

The speed at which you talk plays an important role in determining how well your listener understands you. You have to go about it at an ideal pace so that there is no room for confusion. Lay emphasis on important words that are impactful.

Confidence and Self-Assurance

When you talk, you have to display confidence. You have to be self-assured. If you speak with authority then you will have done half the job. You should be wholehearted and speak honestly. Most people are attracted to these basic qualities.

Vocabulary

When talking to someone, make sure your vocabulary is up to the mark and your audience is able to connect with it the right way. Your vocabulary has to be in good shape to make maximum impact. Try not to use too complex words as that can confuse the audience. Stick with relatable words.

Harmonious Rhythm

Try to make your speech sound harmonious. It should be like notes in a musical piece. You have to time your high note and your low note and add in some short pitches in between to make it interesting and pleasing to the listener.

Some Tips to Improve Your Articulation

Start by imitating your favorite celebrity or public figure you admire and who has a good articulation. This can be talk show hosts, anchors, or radio jockeys etc. whose crisp voice and exciting way of speaking makes them unique.

Record your own voice and practice using recorded audio clips. Make use of audio recordings that have a full range of audacity and makes use of good vocabulary. Listen to it for at least 15 to 30 minutes a day to improve how you sound. Pay attention to all the different details involved.

The power of visualization can help you develop confidence. Right from seeing yourself in front of a large audience, to talking on a television program, can all make you feel like you are capable and can impress any audience. It will help you address your fear and embrace the situation better. It will curb your tension and address your social anxiety. You will feel far less intimidated to approach someone to talk to.

Chapter Five: Expressions

Expressions are important when it comes to putting across a message to a person and making sure that they understand it better. Expressions include vocal range and intonation.

Vocal Range

Vocal range refers to measuring the breadth of the pitch that your voice can phonate. It is usually used in context of singing where a specific characteristic is defined and classified.

It is important for you to identify your vocal range to be able to speak more freely and with much more authority.

It is essential to warm up or exercise your vocal chords in order to vocalize your vocal range. You should be able to go through all the different scales and your entire vocal range, including the scales, thirds and fourths. These will slowly but surely strengthen as you go and set your vocal range boundaries.

In order to enhance the scales, you have to "hum" quite often. It is one of the best ways to exercise your vocal chords. Try to push your limits once in a while and hum for longer periods, but make sure you do not over push it as it can make your voice quite raspy.

Sing regularly. It will help to expand and contract your diaphragm and support your speaking voice.

Using Proper Technique

It is important to use the right techniques in order to enhance your speaking tone as otherwise, you can damage it.

Your larynx should remain at a lower position in order for you to be able to speak openly. To do this, stand straight and draw in a deep breath before exhaling it. Your tongue has to be at the top of your lower teeth and the jaw should be free. Air should consistently flow in and out.

If you wish to speak at a higher range to generate enthusiasm, then force more air through your throat, but make sure you do so gently. It is also a good idea to start a top note so that your vocal chords feel exercised. It will also make sure your voice does not feel too heavy and keep your larynx low and keep it from moving from your chest to your head.

Modifying Vowels and Substitute Words

Sometimes, when speaking, you tend to experience a break or a strain in your voice. Your voice can crack owing to a buildup of tension. In order to avoid this or fix this problem, all you have to do is modify your vowel usage. Try to round off vowel sounds so that you are able to transition from lower notes to higher notes with ease. The next time you try to speak using higher notes, make use of "oo" or "ee" so that it is easier to get your speech going. Change how you stress on vowels to make it sound more scintillating.

If you happen to be working on a challenging note, consider substituting written text with a vocal exercise. Using the word "no" on high notes can help you glide comfortably through the speech. Remember that you have a big vocal range regardless of how your voice sounds or your type of voice. There are usually about 4 to 5 octaves of range involved.

The vocal fry refers to the grunting sound that you make. This sound is tough to control and is usually an auto response. It takes time and effort to garner control over this sound. You will have to work on it consistently, just like you would work on bettering your whistles.

When it comes to having a deeper voice or a chest voice, use techniques such as singing C4-D4-E4-F4-G4, G5-A5-B5-A5-G5 etc.

In order to attain a head voice, mix and control your diaphragm muscles and remember not to put too much stress over your vocal chords as it can damage them.

Whistling is usually the hardest thing to perfect. As you know, you try to whistle a tune thinking you can ace it but often end up making it sound bad. It takes a lot of control to be able to whistle efficiently. It has nothing to do with how much lungpower you need to whistle, and has more to do with the skill required.

Remember to be patient and give your body time to make changes. Practice makes perfect, so you have to put in the effort to learn the new skills and practice them every day.

Conclusion

I thank you once again for choosing this book and hope you had a good time reading it.

The main aim of this book was to help you understand the importance of having a strong speaking voice, and how it can help you defy your shyness to a large extent.

All you have to do is put into practice the different elements mentioned in this book and how you can use them to your advantage.

I urge you to go through this book once more so that you can master your skills and be in a much better position to enhance your speaking voice.

Introvert

Go from Wallflower to Confident Public Speaker in 30 Minutes

By

Stuart Killan

Introduction

Thank you for purchasing this book, 'Shyness: Go from Wallflower to Confident Public Speaker in 30 minutes.'

Over the course of this book, you will learn the importance of public speaking and the strategies you should employ to become a public speaker. Regardless of how well you speak, you must ensure that you know how to impress the audience. If you address the audience about a topic they have no knowledge on, you will lose their attention; therefore, you must know your audience before you write your speech. There are some tips in this book that will help you address some issues that speakers face with their audience.

When someone asked me to speak to an audience, I was terrified. I could feel my heart pounding when I imagined what it would be like to speak to an unknown audience. I felt my body trembling and the blood draining from my face. It often felt like I had a lump in my throat and voice, and that I could never move past that lump, so you can imagine how I felt when someone asked me to do it. I felt like I may faint.

The company I work for hosts a company-wide meeting every two weeks where people discuss the tasks they have worked on. They talk about the results and the outcomes of those tasks. For over three years, I tried my best to avoid going there. I would come up with an excuse a day or two before the meeting. I could never bring myself to imagine speaking to a large audience. That was never going to happen.

Do not get me wrong. I did want to speak to the company and let them know I was working hard to complete my tasks. It was important that the company know what I was doing since it helped improve my career. I wanted to overcome my fear of public speaking since I knew it would do wonders for my career. There will be better opportunities for me to explore since I will make a name for myself in the industry.

However, I never had the courage to do so and I was under the impression that I will make a fool out of myself if I stood in front of a group and spoke. This will hurt my career and make me feel worse than I already do about myself, but there were some techniques that I came across which helped me overcome my fear.

You will learn the importance of public speaking and the strategies you should employ to become a public speaker. Regardless of how well you speak, you must ensure that you know how to impress the audience. If you address the audience about a topic they have no knowledge on, you will lose their attention; therefore, you must know your audience before you write your speech. There are some tips in this book that will help you address some issues that speakers face with their audience.

Over the course of the book, I will provide some information on the different techniques I use to overcome my fear of public speaking. If you use these techniques, you will become an excellent public speaker in 30 minutes or less.

I hope you gather all the information that you are looking for.

Chapter One: How to be a Good Public Speaker

Regardless of whether you talk during a team meeting, or are presenting in front of an audience, you must speak in public from time to time. You can either do well or badly at this, and the outcome affects the way people think about you. It is for this reason that people are anxious if they must speak in public; however, the good news is that when you practice and prepare, you can overcome your anxiety and do well at public speaking. This chapter covers some tips on how you can be an exceptional public speaker.

The Importance of Public Speaking

If you do not have to present to a large group of people, it does not mean that you should not develop public speaking skills. There are many situations where these skills come in handy. These situations help to create opportunities and advance your career.

For instance, you may have to address some students about your company, talk about the work your organization has done at a conference, accept an award or speak to new recruits. You may use visual aids like videos and presentations when you speak to a large audience or when you are training someone.

Public speaking skills are important in many areas of your life. You cannot faint or stutter if your friends ask you to speak at their weddings, or if you must give a eulogy for a family member. You may also need to inspire volunteers to work at a charity event.

In other words, it is important to be a good public speaker to boost your self-confidence, open numerous opportunities and enhance your reputation. If you do not have good skills, you may close doors instead of opening them. For instance, your boss may choose to retract your promotion because you gave a bad presentation. You may also lose a new lead when you give them a bad sales pitch. If you do not look people in the eye and you constantly stutter, you can never make an impression on someone; therefore, you must learn to speak well.

Strategies to Become a Better Speaker

It is easy to learn to be a good public speaker. This section lists some strategies that you can use to become a better presenter and speaker.

Always Plan

It is important that you plan what you are going to say. You can use tools like the 7Cs of Communication, Rhetorical Triangle and Monroe's Motivated Sequence to structure your speech. Once you do this, you should work on the first paragraph. If you wonder why, think about the novel you picked up at the store the other day. If the first paragraph did not interest you, will you bother to read the rest of the book? The same principle applies to your speech too. You should ensure that you intrigue your audience.

For instance, you can begin your speech by talking about something interesting on the news or an interesting statistic. You can also talk about some facts that pertain to the speech you want to give. Storytelling is also a powerful opener, but it takes some practice to know what stories you can tell, and should not tell, when speaking to an audience.

When you plan, you can also think on your feet. This is important since your audience is bound to ask you some questions that you may not have an answer to. You can use your power of communication to answer every question. You should also remember that you could schedule every occasion where you need to speak in public. You should learn to make good impromptu speeches. Prepare mini speeches or have ideas about what you can say if you should address the crowd. You should also ensure that you have a thorough understanding of what happens within your organization.

Practice

It is true that practice makes you perfect. You cannot be a compelling or confident speaker if you do not practice. You must seek opportunities where you can speak to a large audience. For example, you can join the Toastmasters club where you will meet other aspiring speakers. You can practice to your heart's content at Toastmasters' sessions. You can also ensure that you are in a situation where you should speak in public, like taking up the opportunity to join the cross-training program in your organization, or volunteering to conduct activities for the employees in your organization.

If you are going to deliver a speech or presentation, you should create it as soon as you can. When you put it together earlier, you have more time to practice. You can practice this speech plenty of times when you are alone, or use your friends as your audience. Ask them for feedback and tweak your speech to ensure that you do not stumble or stutter in between.

You can try to run the speech past a dummy audience to help you calm your nerves. This will make you feel more comfortable with your material. You can also use the feedback that your audience gives you to enhance your performance.

Engage the Audience

Regardless of the topic you choose to speak on, you must engage your audience. When you engage the audience, you will not worry about being the only one speaking since you will involve everyone when you deliver your message. You can also ask the audience some questions if it is appropriate to encourage their participation.

You should keep in mind that there are some words that can reduce your power when you speak. For example, think of how the following sentences resonate within you – "I want to add that we can think of meeting these goals" or "I think this is a great plan." The word 'think' limits your conviction and authority. Try to avoid using them when you address a crowd.

"Actually" is another word you should avoid. When someone says, "I would like to add that we were actually under stress last quarter." When you use this word, it shows the people around you that you are submissive and may come as a surprise to them. Instead, you can say, "We were under a lot of stress last quarter."

You must also pay attention to how you speak. If you are nervous, you will rush through your speech since you want to walk off stage as fast as you can. You may trip on your words and say things you do not mean. Try to take deep breaths and force yourself to slow down. Do not be afraid to gather your thoughts since it is a good idea to pause and let the information sink in. This will make you seem more natural, confident and authentic.

You should also avoid reading your speech word-for-word from a piece of paper or notes. You can make a list of the important points on flash cards or cue cards. When you get better at public speaking, try to memorize the whole speech. You can always refer to your cue cards if you need to.

Body Language Matters

Your body language gives the audience an idea of how you feel inside. You may be unaware of it, but how you move your hands or stand makes an impact on your speech. If you are nervous and do not believe a word of what you are saying, your stance will say it all. The audience will know that you are lying to them. Pay attention to your body language. Look people in the eye, stand up straight, smile and take deep breaths. Avoid leaning on one leg, or using gestures that do not come naturally to you.

Most people like to stand behind a podium if they must speak in public or give a presentation. These podiums can be used to hold your cue cards; however, they create a barrier between you and the audience. You can also use this place to hide from the audience.

Instead of standing behind the podium while you speak, try to walk around the stage and use gestures to engage the audience. This movement will also allow your voice to come through, making your speech more passionate and active.

Think Positively

When you think positively, you can increase your confidence. When you are afraid, you will constantly tell yourself that you are a failure and the cycle of negative self-talk comes into play. This happens a few minutes before you should speak in public. If you tell yourself that you are going to make a fool out of yourself, or that you are going to fall the minute you step on stage, you are not helping yourself. This self-sabotaging talk lowers your confidence and increases the probability that you will never achieve anything.

You can use affirmations and visualizations to increase your confidence. This is especially important to do right before your presentation or speech. Try to visualize that you are going to give a successful presentation and imagine how great you will feel when people comment on how well you have done. Always use positive affirmations to build your confidence.

Cope with Nerves

Have you ever watched or listened to a speaker who messed up his speech? The chances of that happening are very rare. When you must speak in public, you only visualize all the terrible things that can happen to you. You tell yourself that you will forget everything you want to say and will pass out of nervousness. This makes you worry about whether you will lose your job or not, but these situations never arise. You only build these in your mind and become more nervous than you have any reason to be.

Many people will tell you that they are afraid to address a large audience. This fear is due to their fear of failing. When you speak in public, your fight or flight response kicks in. The endocrine system secretes large volumes of adrenaline, which courses through your bloodstream. It makes you sweat, makes your heart beat faster and makes you breathe faster.

These symptoms can be debilitating and annoying, but they can enhance your performance if you use the nervous energy to your advantage.

You must first stop thinking about your nervousness, fear and yourself. You should only focus on the audience and remember that whatever you are saying is for them alone. Through your speech, you are trying to educate the audience, or help them in some way; therefore, your message should resonate confidence and not fear. You should focus on what the audience wants, instead of worrying about your needs.

If you have some time before your speech, practice some breathing exercises that will give your body enough oxygen. This will help to slow your heart rate down too. It is important that you perform these exercises before you speak. Take a deep breath and hold it for several seconds before you exhale slowly.

It is true that a crowd is more intimidating when compared to individuals; therefore, try to think of the crowd as an individual. You can also focus on a friend of yours in the crowd and talk to the crowd as if only your friend is in the room.

Exercise to Stay Calm

Since you know when you must address an audience, you can plan your day in advance. You should try to workout at least three hours before your speech. You can take a stroll in the park too. Studies have concluded that exercise helps to alleviate stress and anxiety. When you exercise, your body releases endorphins which make you feel better. Your body temperature also increases which helps to keep you calm. You stop worrying about the speech and will be more confident about interacting with a large audience. If you are still nervous before the speech, run around the room to ensure that your body releases some endorphins.

Transform Your Nervous Energy into Positive Energy

This tip is similar to the one mentioned above. Some speakers listen to loud music or drink an energy drink before they give a speech. This helps them turn their nervous energy into positive energy. Many studies have concluded that a speaker can win over the audience and make an eloquent speech if he is enthusiastic. Your body may react differently to caffeine. Therefore, ensure that you do not overdose on caffeine.

Record Your Speeches and Watch Them.

If you can record your speeches and presentations, do it. You will find it easier to improve your speaking skills when you watch yourself later. This will help you work on the areas that did not work well with the audience. While you watch the speech, notice the number of times you stalled by saying "like" or "um."

Look at your body language – are you leaning against the podium, did you only stand behind the podium, are you swaying, etc. Check whether you smiled at your audience and looked at them as often as you could. Did you enunciate well? Look at your gestures – do they look forced? Did people notice the gestures you were making if you only stood behind the podium? Now, look at how you handled yourself when the audience interrupted you. Was there a question you did not prepare for, or did someone sneeze? Did you look surprised, annoyed or hesitant when the audience asked you a question? Make notes and try to work on these points when you make your next speech.

Chapter Two: How to Impress Your Audience

There are some speakers whose speeches enthrall and interest you, and their words resonate within you for a long time, so what is it that makes them better speakers? Do you think it is their personality, intelligence, confidence, experience and lack of anxiety, or a mix of all these traits? It can be any of the traits mentioned earlier. Speakers often rely on some principles of social, applied and educational psychology. They focus only on their audience and do justice to their speech by giving the audience what they want. Let me give you an example on why it is important for a speaker to know his audience well.

I attended a sales conference early this year where I sat through a speech given by two young men. They were trying to sell a product that they had developed. At the end of their speech, they asked the audience if they would like to purchase their product. Few people volunteered since the young men were unable to grasp the attention of the audience. They only made $3,000 that day.

I approached these gentlemen after their speech and asked them how they felt about it. They were honest and told me that they thought their speech was terrible and that they had no time to practice. I told them to engage the audience during break and during their speech. They decided to use this advice and started speaking to the people in the room during break.

They requested for some time the following day to address the audience again. They did a splendid job with their speech and sold $40,000 worth of the product! Some of the tips I had given them are listed in this chapter.

Always Know Your Audience

Before you give a speech, you should understand the knowledge that the audience has about the topic. You must understand if they are familiar with the topic and identify what they want out of the session. When you do your homework ahead of time, you will know what to say and can anticipate some questions that the audience may ask you.

You should start the discussion off by asking the audience some simple questions. You can either ask them to raise their hands or answer. This ensures that their limbs are active and helps you assess the intelligence of the audience. You can then adjust your speech to cater to the audience's needs. Let us assume that you should address the children in a high school on career day. You must ensure that you know the number of students who have information about the career you are going to talk about.

Focus on the Audience

You must focus on your audience. A charismatic speaker always uses eye contact to impress the crowd. They scan the crowd when they begin their speech, and then choose the people in the audience whom they can look right in the eye. They are communicating to that member in the audience that they are talking to them. The audience will immediately connect with the speaker and value their opinion. It is important that you look at the people in the back of the audience too, or at least pretend that you are looking at them. You must draw everyone into the circle and ensure that they do not look away when you speak to them.

Use Visual Aids Wisely

You can use multiple visual aids like PowerPoint or videos when you make your speech, but people often misuse these tools. The best presentations are those that are short, crisp and clean. If you have graphics to illustrate your points or concepts, you can use them to explain to the audience. Most people try to cram a lot of information on the slides, and do their best to read the information in the slides of the presentation. Instead, you should use bullet points in every slide and restrict the number to four points per slide. If there is a point on the slide, it is for your audience to read it and not for you.

Stop Reading Your Speech

As mentioned earlier, you should avoid reading the speech from a piece of paper. You do not have to use all the words that you have written on the sheet. The problem with this approach is that people will prefer not to attend your speeches. They may ask you to share your speech with them via email instead of listening to you give it. You should remember that they want to hear you give your take on the topic and are waiting for you to give it in person; therefore, you must make it worth their effort and time. As an example, think of the speeches that Academy Award winners give. The recipients of the award never read their speech. If your eyes are glued to your paper, you can never grasp the attention of the audience.

Do Not Force Humor

Most people are not funny when they read a joke. They are funny when they react to a situation that is happening at that moment. For example, when you make comments about yourself after you made a mistake in your speech, the audience will snigger because you did not write that joke down. It came to you instantly. You can also react to situations where someone from the audience made a comment or there was a noise in the hallway. NEVER try to make fun of a member in the audience. You are not there to entertain the crowd, and you are certainly not a stand-up comic. If you are the latter, you must ensure that you are good at pacifying the crowd if you make fun of them.

Focus on the Now

Always focus on the current situation. Funny situations become funnier when they evolve. You will be a great speaker when you focus on what you are saying, and how the audience is reacting to what you are saying. You will also find that you are less nervous when you understand the content that you are presenting. Ensure that you do not focus on how nervous you are, and how you would love to get out of there. There are some experts who suggest that people should just go with the flow when they are speaking to an audience. You must strike a balance between your fear and your need to look calm.

Decide What You Want to Say

You must decide what you can say in the time that is given to you, and then reduce the speech by half. There may have been times when you apologized to the audience that you had more to say to them, but did not have enough time to do so. I have done the same too, on many occasions. The only way you can ensure that you cover all the information you want to share with the crowd is by removing some unnecessary points and sentences from your speech. That way you can ensure that you have some points that you can cover if there is more time left. Your audience will appreciate it if you end your speech early since that gives them enough time to answer your questions. Do not worry about removing some information since it is better to have some time left at the end of the speech.

Give Yourself Time Points

Let us assume that you have thirty minutes to address the audience. Make a list of the points you want to cover within 15 minutes, 20 minutes and ensure that you end your speech in 25 minutes. This gives the audience enough time to ask you questions. While you draft your speech, you can work backward and see what points you want to cover in the beginning and end. Regardless of the method you apply, it is important that you set a timeline for yourself. This will help you pace your speech. If someone sends you a message that you only have five minutes left until the end of your speech, you should not panic. When you pace yourself, you can reduce the speed at which you talk. This allows you to emphasize on the points in your speech.

Always Practice

If you are not an entertainer and find it difficult to speak to an audience, you should practice your speech a few times before you address the crowd. This has been mentioned earlier.

Public speaking is not an art, but a science, since you follow a set of rules that will help you address the crowd. Of course, there is some art to it since you will find it difficult to win the crowd over when you do not have charisma. The rules mentioned in this chapter will help you grasp the attention of your audience, and make you a great speaker. It is important to remember that your personal traits and qualities make the speech come together. You have to use your uniqueness to keep the audience hooked to your speech.

Conclusion

Thank you for purchasing this book.

Most people are afraid to address a crowd since they worry about how the crowd will feel about them; therefore, it becomes harder for them to speak in public since they constantly worry about their image. This fear makes it hard for them to visualize a situation where they should speak to the public. This fear is often irrational since people always imagine the worst-case scenarios; however, public speaking is not difficult if you have some tricks up your sleeve.

It is important to remember that you practice your speeches and grab every opportunity to speak in public. I hope you become a great orator and impress your audience with your speeches.

Made in the USA
Monee, IL
06 July 2021